ENGLISH
900

ENGLISH
900
BOOK THREE

prepared by
ENGLISH LANGUAGE SERVICES, INC.
Washington, D.C.

The Macmillan Company, New York
Collier-Macmillan Limited, London
Collier-Macmillan Canada, Ltd.

The Macmillan Company, New York
Collier-Macmillan Canada, Ltd., Toronto, Ontario

Printed in the United States of America

5F

PREFACE

ENGLISH 900, a course for adult students of English as a second language, contains material from beginning through intermediate levels of study. The whole series consists of textbooks, workbooks, and tape recordings, with a teacher's handbook.

ENGLISH 900 is one of the basic instructional courses in the Collier-Macmillan English Program. Included in the Program is a series of graded readers in which five are keyed to the vocabulary and structure of each study unit in the basic texts of ENGLISH 900.

The series takes its name from the 900 base sentences presented in the six textbooks. The sentences cover the basic structures and a basic vocabulary of the English language. They are introduced at the rate of fifteen in each study unit, or a hundred and fifty in each book, and are numbered consecutively from Base Sentence 1 in the first unit of Book One through Base Sentence 900 in the last unit of Book Six. These structures provide "building blocks" for all of the material studied in the series, e.g., there are approximately four variation sentences for each base sentence. As a part of his mastery of English, therefore, the student practices and learns approximately 3,600 variation sentences in addition to the basic 900 patterns.

There are ten study units in each textbook in the series. Each study unit contains a group of fifteen base sentences related to a meaningful situation. In Book One of the series, the typical study unit begins with the presentation of the fifteen *Base Sentences* together with *Intonation* patterns. *Questions and Answers* follow and give the student practice in pairing and matching the base sentences into conversational form. *Substitution Drills* introduce the variation sentences, using vocabulary and grammatical substitution techniques. These early sections of the unit provide the pronunciation practice and drill material needed for the mastery of language forms. The *Conversation* section consists of short dialogues giving the student the opportunity to practice the new lesson material in informal conversation in the classroom. *Exercises* in each unit can be used as oral and written drills for all of the materials introduced in the unit.

Units in the succeeding books in the series (Books Two to Six) contain Base Sentences, Intonation practice, Substitution Drills, Conversation, and Exercises, and, in addition, certain new features. Beginning with Book Two, a *Reading Practice* section is added to each unit, and, beginning with Book Three, a *Verb Study* section. Books Four, Five, and Six include *Participation Drills* for classroom use, and Books Five and Six present *Grammar Study* materials and *review exercises*.

Each textbook includes a *Key* to the exercises and a *Word Index* which lists in alphabetical order every word introduced in the book, and cites the sentence and unit number in which the new word first occurred. There are special *Review Units* in Books One through Four.

A companion Workbook is available for each of the six textbooks, and a series of 180 pre-recorded tapes has been prepared for language laboratory use. ENGLISH 900 Workbooks are unique in that they have been programmed for use by the student as home study material to reinforce classroom work. The Workbooks "test" the student on the textbook materials, and review the important points in each unit that he may not have mastered in class.

For classes that meet for three to five hours a week, each textbook in the series provides material for approximately three months of study. Suggestions for teaching the course, as well as detailed descriptions of all of the materials in ENGLISH 900, have been given in the Teacher's Manual which accompanies the series.

A wide range of material has been created for the Collier-Macmillan English Program by the Materials Development Staff of English Language Services, Inc., under the co-direction of Edwin T. Cornelius, Jr., and Willard D. Sheeler. ENGLISH 900 was prepared under the direction of Edwin T. Cornelius, Jr., with Joyce Manes as Project Editor.

CONTENTS

The numbers of the Base Sentences in each unit follow the unit titles.

UNIT 1 DESCRIBING OBJECTS

301 What color is your book?

302 My book has a dark blue cover.

303 How much does that typewriter weigh?

304 It's not too heavy, but I don't know the exact weight.

305 This round table weighs about forty-five pounds.

306 What size suitcase do you own?

307 One of my suitcases is small, and the other one is medium size.

308 I like the shape of that table.

309 How long is Jones Boulevard?

310 That street is only two miles long.

311 Will you please measure this window to see how wide it is?

312 This window is just as wide as that one.

313 The walls are three inches thick.

314 This material feels soft.

315 This pencil is longer than that one.

1

INTONATION

301   What color is your book?

302   My book has a dark blue cover.

303   How much does that typewriter weigh?

304   It's not too heavy, but I don't know the exact weight.

305   This round table weighs about forty-five pounds.

306   What size suitcase do you own?

307   One of my suitcases is small, and the other one is medium size.

308   I like the shape of that table.

309   How long is Jones Boulevard?

310   That street is only two miles long.

311   Will you please measure this window to see how wide it is?

312   This window is just as wide as that one.

313   The walls are three inches thick.

314   This material feels soft.

315   This pencil is longer than that one.

VERB STUDY

1. **weigh**
   a. How much does that typewriter weigh?
   b. This table weighs about forty-five pounds.
   c. Did you weigh the suitcase?
   d. Yes, I weighed the suitcase this morning.

2. **like**
   a. I like the shape of that table.
   b. Do you like the shape of that window?
   c. I liked the movie very much.
   d. He likes the medium size suitcase.

3. **measure**
   a. Will you please measure this window?
   b. I've already measured that window.
   c. I'm measuring the window right now.
   d. Did he measure the table to see how long it is?

4. **feel**
   a. This material feels soft.
   b. I feel fine today.
   c. I didn't feel well yesterday.
   d. He felt the material to see how soft it was.

5. **own**
   a. What size suitcase do you own?
   b. I own a small suitcase and a medium size one.
   c. He owns that automobile.
   d. Last year he owned a good automobile.

6. **have**
   a. My book has a dark blue cover.
   b. I have two suitcases.
   c. Last year I had a good typewriter.
   d. Does he have a dark blue book?

7. **be**
   a. What color is your book?
   b. The walls are three inches thick.
   c. I'm a doctor.
   d. He was in New York yesterday.
   e. Isn't John your brother?

SUBSTITUTION DRILLS

1. What color is your | book / pencil / typewriter / camera | ? Do you remember?

2. My book has a | dark blue / light blue / bright red / red and blue | cover. Have you seen it?

3. How much does that | typewriter / table / dog / elephant | weigh? Can you tell me?

4. It's | not too heavy / not awfully heavy / very light / pretty light / fairly heavy | , but I don't know the exact weight.

5. This | round / square / long / narrow / small | table weighs about forty-five pounds.

6. What size | suitcase / notebook / house / apartment / diamond | do you own?

7. One of my suitcases is | small / large / little / big | , and the other one is medium.

8. I like the | shape | of that table. Do you like it?
                 size
                 color
                 weight

9. How | long | is Jones Boulevard? Do you know?
          wide
          narrow
          big

10. That street is only | two miles long | . What's the name of
                           two blocks long   the street?
                           300 yards long
                           two miles in length
                           900 feet long

11. Will you please measure this window to see how | wide | it is?
                                                       narrow
                                                       high
                                                       big
                                                       small

12. This window is just as | wide | as that one.
                              narrow
                              high
                              big
                              small
                              high and wide

13. The walls are | three inches | thick. How high are the walls?
                     two feet
                     one yard
                     3 in.
                     2 ft.
                     1 yd.

14. This material feels
soft
hard
wet
dry
hard and dry
soft and wet

. How does that material feel?

15. This pencil is
longer
shorter
bigger
smaller
heavier
lighter

than that one.

16. This book weighs
two pounds
twenty ounces
2 lbs.
25 oz.

. What's the weight of that book?

17. This window is
two feet
twenty-six inches
2'
26"

wide. What's the width of that window?

18.
What size
How big

is your apartment?

19. Do you
have
own
want

a large suitcase?

20. Your suitcase
is
looks
feels

very heavy.

READING PRACTICE

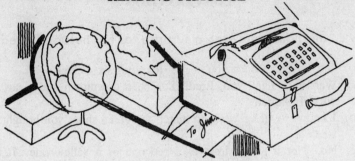

Describing Objects

Yesterday was Jim's birthday. He got a lot of presents from his friends and family. All the gifts were wrapped in colored paper. Some of the packages were large, but others were very small. Some were heavy, and others were light. One square package was blue; there was a book in it. Another one was long and narrow; it had an umbrella in it. Jim's sister gave him a big, round package. He thought it was a ball, but it was not. When he removed the yellow paper that covered it, he saw that it was a globe of the world.

After that his brother gave Jim another gift. It was a big box wrapped in green paper. Jim opened it and found another box covered with red paper. He removed the paper and saw a third box; this one was blue in color.

Everyone laughed as Jim opened the boxes. There were six of them! In the last one he found a small white envelope. There was a piece of paper in the envelope which said: "Go to the big bedroom. Look in the closet near the high window. You will see three suitcases: a black one, a brown one and a gray one. Your birthday present is in one of these."

Jim went in the large bedroom. He went to the closet and began opening the suitcases. He had to open all of them before he saw his brother's present. He was very happy. It was just what Jim wanted—a portable typewriter.

Questions

1. What was in the square blue package?
2. What did Jim's sister give him?
3. What was in the long, narrow box?
4. Describe the gift from Jim's brother.
5. Was Jim happy with the gift from his brother? Why?

CONVERSATION

Judy comes home late with a surprise for her husband, Fred.

FRED: Judy! Where have you been? It's after six o'clock.

JUDY: Wait until I tell you, Fred! I've been downtown and I saw just what I wanted.

FRED: I know. A green dress to match the green shoes you bought last week.

JUDY: No. Not a green dress or a red one or a yellow one. It isn't anything for me. It's for our house.

FRED: Our house? What is it?

JUDY: You'll never guess. It's a new sofa. A yellow one.

FRED: We already have a sofa, Judy. A very good one.

JUDY: I never liked it. It's brown and our other furniture is light blue. It doesn't match. The yellow one will look good with our other things.

FRED: Very well. Tell me about it.

JUDY: First of all, it's exactly the right size for the wall near the window. The sofa we have now is too short.

FRED: Is it wide or narrow?

JUDY: It's as wide as our old sofa, but it looks narrower because it's longer.

FRED: Fine. Then I'll have a very good place to sleep after dinner.

EXERCISES

1. Complete the following sentences with the correct word.

   Example: My automobile is *longer* than yours. (*longer, length, medium, small*)

   a. This typewriter weighs _____. (*light, heavy, 25 lbs., 10 inches*)

   b. The typewriter is _____ than this pencil. (*light, heavy, lighter, heavier*)

   c. This pencil is _____ than the typewriter. (*light, heavy, lighter, heavier*)

   d. Jones Boulevard measures _____ in width. (*36 lbs., heavy, 36 oz., 36 feet*)

   e. It is _____ than Lane Street. (*wide, wider, width, weight*)

   f. I don't know the exact _____ of the window. (*wide, wider, width, high*)

   g. This window is _____ than that one. (*narrow, narrower, height, width*)

   h. This wall is just as _____ as that one. (*thick, thickness, width, height*)

2. Complete the sentences with the correct word from the list below:

   weight   size   color   shape   length
   height   width   material

   a. The _____ of this book is blue.

   b. The _____ of this table is round.

   c. The _____ of this suitcase is 20 lbs.

   d. The _____ of the street is 2 miles.

   e. This suitcase is a small _____.

   f. This window is high. Its _____ is three feet.

   g. This is a wide street. Its _____ is 36 feet.

   h. This _____ feels soft.

3. Complete the sentences below with the appropriate words from the list:

large	wide	long	light	hard
narrow	thick	soft	small	dry
thin	heavy	wet	short	

Example: Elephants are big. They are not *small*.

a. This suitcase is awfully heavy. It is not _____.

b. This table is pretty small. It is not _____.

c. This material feels fairly soft. It is not _____.

d. Jones Boulevard is very wide. It is not _____.

e. The window was wet. It was not _____.

f. These walls are two feet thick. They are not _____.

g. This street is very long. It is not _____.

h. This is a thin book. It is not _____.

i. This is a narrow window. It is not _____.

j. This is a light briefcase. It is not _____.

k. This is a hard bed. It is not _____.

l. This street is dry. It is not _____.

m. This table is short. It is not _____.

4. Complete the questions with one of the expressions from the list below:

how wide	how long	what is the weight
how thick	what color	what is the thickness
what sizes	what shape	what is the width
how much heavier	what is the length	how tall

Example: *What is the width* of that window? It is 3 feet wide.

a. _____ of that pencil? It weighs 2 oz.

b. _____ is that window? It is 41 inches in width.

c. _____ is that street? It is two miles in length.

d. _____ is that wall? It is three feet thick.

e. _____ of that street? It is 36 feet wide.

f. _____ is this book than that one? They are the same weight.

g. _____ is your book? It is red and blue.

h. _____ are your suitcases? One is small and the other is medium.

i. _____ is that table? It is round.

j. _____ of that material? It is three yards long.

k. _____ is John? His height is exactly six feet.

5. **Use the right verb form:**

   weighing   weigh   weighs   am   is   are
   measure   measures   measuring

   a. How many pounds do you _____?

   b. I don't know how many pounds I _____.

   c. John _____ one hundred and fifty pounds.

   d. You _____ your suitcase to see what size it is.

   e. My mother _____ the windows to see how wide they are.

   f. I _____ heavier than my sister.

   g. These windows _____ wider than those.

   h. Dogs _____ smaller than elephants.

   i. How much does that typewriter _____?

   j. They are _____ the windows now to see how high they are.

   k. I am _____ my suitcase to see what its weight is.

   l. The boulevard _____ only three miles long.

   m. That man is _____ the boulevard now to see what its width is.

   n. That street _____ longer than this one.

   o. Will you _____ the length of this material for me, please?

WORD LIST

apartment	high	short, shorter, shortest
as . . . as	inch	size
awfully	large	small, smaller, smallest
big, bigger, biggest	length	soft
bright	light, lighter, lightest	square
camera	long, longer, longest	suitcase
color	material	thick
cover	medium	too
dark	mile	typewriter
diamond	narrow	weight
elephant	only	wet
fairly	ounce	wide
foot, feet	pound	width
hard	round	yard
heavy, heavier, heaviest	shape	

Verb Forms

p. = past; p. part. = past participle
feel, felt (*p. and p. part.*)
measure, measured (*p. and p. part.*)
own, owned (*p. and p. part.*)
weigh, weighed (*p. and p. part.*)

Expression

how much

Weights and Measures

26″ = twenty-six inches
26 in. = twenty-six inches
2′ = two feet
2 ft. = two feet
1 yd. = one yard
25 oz. = twenty-five ounces
2 lb. = two pounds

Supplementary Word List

(Conversation and Reading Practice)

ball	furniture	removed
bedroom	gifts	shoes
box	globe	sofa
closet	laughed	surprise
colored	match	umbrella
covered	package	why
downtown	portable	wrapped
dress	presents	

UNIT 2 ASKING PEOPLE TO DO THINGS

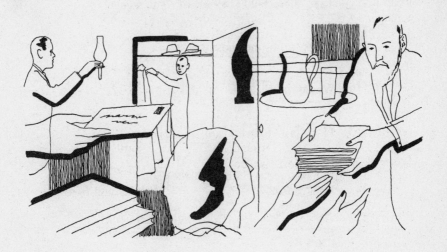

316   Would you please tell Mr. Cooper that I'm here?

317   Take these books home with you tonight.

318   Please bring me those magazines.

319   Would you help me lift this heavy box?

320   Please ask John to turn on the lights.

321   Put your books down on the table.

322   Get me a hammer from the kitchen, will you?

323   Hang up my coat in the closet, will you please?

324   Please don't bother me now. I'm very busy.

325   Would you mind mailing this letter for me?

326   If you have time, will you call me tomorrow?

327   Please pick up those cups and saucers.

328   Will you do me a favor?

329   Please count the chairs in that room.

330   Please pour this milk into that glass.

INTONATION

316   Would you please tell Mr. Cooper that I'm here?

317   Take these books home with you tonight.

318   Please bring me those magazines.

319   Would you help me lift this heavy box?

320   Please ask John to turn on the lights.

321   Put your books down on the table.

322   Get me a hammer from the kitchen, will you?

323   Hang up my coat in the closet, will you please?

324   Please don't bother me now. I'm very busy.

325   Would you mind mailing this letter for me?

326   If you have time, will you call me tomorrow?

327   Please pick up those cups and saucers.

328   Will you do me a favor?

329   Please count the chairs in that room.

330   Please pour this milk into that glass.

VERB STUDY

1. **tell, ask**
   - *a.* Please tell Mr. Cooper that I'm here.
   - *b.* I've already told him.
   - *c.* Please ask John to help me.
   - *d.* I've already asked John to help you.

2. **take, bring, get**
   - *a.* Take these books home with you tonight.
   - *b.* I took those books home with me last night.
   - *c.* Please bring me those magazines.
   - *d.* He brought me two magazines.
   - *e.* Get me a hammer from the kitchen, will you?
   - *f.* He got me a hammer from the kitchen.

3. **turn on, turn off**
   - *a.* Please ask John to turn on the lights.
   - *b.* John already turned on the lights.
   - *c.* Please ask John to turn off the lights.
   - *d.* John already turned off the lights.

4. **pick up, put down, hang up**
   - *a.* Please pick up those cups and saucers.
   - *b.* He already picked up those cups and saucers.
   - *c.* Please put your books down.
   - *d.* I've already put my books down.
   - *e.* Hang up my coat, will you please?
   - *f.* He hung up my coat in the closet.

5. **bother, help**
   - *a.* Please don't bother me now.
   - *b.* Is he bothering you?
   - *c.* Would you help me?
   - *d.* He helped me lift the heavy box.

6. **count**
   - *a.* Please count the chairs in that room.
   - *b.* I've already counted the chairs in that room.

7. **pour**
   - *a.* Please pour this milk into that glass.
   - *b.* I've already poured the milk into the glass.

8. **call**
   - *a.* If you have time, will you call me tomorrow?
   - *b.* He called me last night.

SUBSTITUTION DRILLS

1. Would you please | tell him | that I'm here?
   - advise him
   - let him know
   - remind him

2. Take these books | home | with you tonight.
   - to the meeting
   - to the library

3. Please | bring | me those magazines. They're not very heavy.
   - give
   - hand
   - throw

4. Would you help me | lift | this heavy box?
   - carry
   - move
   - wrap
   - weigh
   - measure

5. Please ask John to | turn on the lights | .
   - turn off the lights
   - turn the lights on
   - turn the lights off

6. | Put your books down | on the table, will you please?
   - Put down your books
   - Put your books
   - Leave your books
   - Place your books

7. Get me | a hammer | from the kitchen, will you?
   - a nail
   - a ruler
   - a yardstick

8. | Hang up my coat | in the closet, will you?
   - Hang my coat up
   - Put my coat
   - Leave my coat
   - Put my coat back

9. Please don't | bother | me now. I'm very busy.
   - interrupt
   - talk to
   - argue with

10. Would you mind | mailing this letter | for me? I'm busy this
    - mailing this package | afternoon.
    - wrapping this package
    - calling Mr. Cooper

11. If you have time, will you | call | me tomorrow?
    - visit
    - come to see
    - do a favor for
    - mail a letter for

12. Please pick up those | cups and saucers | , will you?
    - plates and glasses
    - knives and forks
    - spoons

13. Will | you | do me a favor? I'm very busy this afternoon.
    - he
    - she
    - they

14. Please count | the chairs | in that room. How many are there?
    - the desks
    - the pictures
    - the rugs

15. | Would you please pour | this milk into that glass?
    - Will you please pour
    - Could you please pour
    - Would you mind pouring

16. Would you please ask John to | hang my coat up | ?
    - get me a hammer
    - take back these books
    - bring me those magazines

17. | If you have time | , will you call me tomorrow?
    - If you are able to
    - If you think of it

READING PRACTICE

Asking People To Do Things

When Henry Allen came home from the office last Thursday night he saw a note from his wife on the kitchen table. "Henry," the note said, "my mother isn't well and I am going home to be with her for a few days. There are a few things that ought to be done while I'm away.

"First, take your blue coat to the dry cleaner's and leave your shirts at the laundry. At the same time, would you please stop at the shoe repairman's and get my brown shoes? And go to the supermarket and get some coffee, milk, and butter.

"When you get home, please telephone Mary Bickford and tell her I won't be able to go to her party tomorrow evening. Tell her why I can't come.

"There are three things that must be done before you go to work tomorrow morning: leave a note for the milkman asking for just one quart of milk, not two; put the garbage in the backyard; give the dog something to eat.

"If you have time on Saturday, cut the grass. Don't forget the grass in the backyard. The newspaper boy will come on Saturday afternoon. Be sure to give him money.

"I think that's all. I'll telephone this evening and let you know how Mother is.

Love,
Alice"

Henry looked out the window at the grass Alice wanted him to cut. His wife had asked him to do many things. He hoped her mother would be well very quickly.

Questions

1. What did Henry find on the kitchen table?
2. Where had Alice gone? Why?
3. What was the first thing Alice wanted Henry to do?
4. Why did Henry have to telephone Mary?
5. What did Alice ask Henry to do on Saturday if he had time?

CONVERSATION

1. Frank asks Tom to help him.

FRANK: Would you mind helping me for a minute, Tom?

TOM: I'd be glad to, Frank. What do you want me to do?

FRANK: Help me hang up this picture. Hold it straight while I put in the nail.

TOM: I'd be glad to.

FRANK: Hand me the hammer. Give me one of those nails, too, please.

TOM: Here you are.

FRANK: There. How does that look? Tell me if I have it straight.

TOM: Yes, it's straight, but it's upside down.

2. Ella prepares a birthday cake.

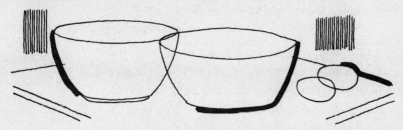

ELLA: Will you bring me two eggs from the refrigerator, Barbara?

BARBARA: Here are the eggs. Anything else I can do for you?

ELLA: Yes. Put the egg whites in one bowl and the yolks in another.

BARBARA: What are you making? A cake?

ELLA: That's right. Don't tell Harry. It's for his birthday. Keep it a secret.

BARBARA: I won't tell anyone.

EXERCISES

1. Complete the following sentences with the appropriate words from the list below:

doing for   hang up   turn on   put down
wait for   pick up   turn off   taking back

   a. Please ask John to _____ the lights _____. It's dark in here.

   b. _____ your books _____ on the table, please.

   c. _____ my coat _____ in the closet, will you?

   d. Please don't _____ me. I'll be busy all afternoon.

   e. Would you mind _____ a favor _____ me?

   f. Would you please _____ those cups and saucers from the table?

   g. Would you mind _____ these books_____ to the library?

   h. Tell him to _____ the lights _____ when he goes to bed.

2. Change the following to questions using the expression "Would you please . . ." Follow the example.

   Example: I want you to turn on the lights.
   Would you please turn on the lights?

   a. I want you to get me a hammer.
   b. I want you to count the chairs in this room.
   c. I want you to pour this milk into that glass.
   d. I want you to help me lift this heavy box.
   e. I want you to take these books home.
   f. I want you to turn the lights off.
   g. I want you to bring me those magazines.

3. Complete the following sentences with the correct form of the word in parentheses.

   Examples: Please *bring* me the magazine. (*bring*)
   Would you mind *bringing* me the magazine? (*bring*)
   Ask John to *bring* me the magazine. (*bring*)

a. Would you please _____ me wrap this box? (*help*)

b. Would you mind _____ me wrap this box? (*help*)

c. Please don't _____ me wrap this box. (*help*)

d. Would you ask John to _____ me wrap this box? (*help*)

e. Would you please _____ this letter for me? (*mail*)

f. Would you mind _____ this letter for me? (*mail*)

g. Please don't _____ this letter for me. (*mail*)

h. Ask John to _____ this letter for me. (*mail*)

i. Would you please _____ your coat up? (*hang*)

j. Would you mind _____ your coat up? (*hang*)

k. Please don't _____ up your coat. (*hang*)

l. Would you ask John to _____ his coat up? (*hang*)

4. **Change the following to negative sentences.**

Examples: I am a doctor. *I'm not a doctor.*
Bring me a glass of milk. *Don't bring me a glass of milk.*

a. Wait for me at five o'clock.
b. She'll have time to do me a favor.
c. He got me a glass of milk yesterday.
d. Are you going to help me wrap this box?
e. Bring me a yardstick.
f. These nails weigh too much.
g. I turned off the radio.
h. I am very busy.
i. Pour me a cup of coffee.
j. He helped me lift the heavy box.
k. Count all the chairs in this room.
l. He is bothering me.
m. Is he talking to you?
n. Take these magazines back to the library.
o. Leave your books on the table.

WORD LIST

box	kitchen	package	saucer
closet	knife, knives	picture	spoon
fork	library	plate	that
hammer	light	rug	yardstick
into	nail	ruler	

Verb Forms

advise, advised (*p. and p. part.*)
argue, argued (*p. and p. part.*)
bother, bothered (*p. and p. part.*)
bring, brought (*p. and p. part.*)
carry, carried (*p. and p. part.*)
count, counted (*p. and p. part.*)
hand, handed (*p. and p. part.*)
hang up, hung up (*p. and p. part.*)
help, helped (*p. and p. part.*)
interrupt, interrupted (*p. and p. part.*)
let (someone) know, let (someone) know (*p. and p. part.*)
lift, lifted (*p. and p. part.*)
mail, mailed (*p. and p. part.*)
move, moved (*p. and p. part.*)
pick up, picked up (*p. and p. part.*)

place, placed (*p. and p. part.*)
pour, poured (*p. and p. part.*)

put, put (*p. and p. part.*)
put back, put back (*p. and p. part.*)
put down, put down (*p. and p. part.*)
remind, reminded (*p. and p. part.*)

take, took (*p.*), taken (*p. part.*)
take back, took back (*p.*), taken back (*p. part.*)

throw, threw (*p.*), thrown (*p. part.*)
turn off, turned off (*p. and p. part.*)
turn on, turned on (*p. and p. part.*)
wrap, wrapped (*p. and p. part.*)

Expressions

be able to
do a favor (for)

Supplementary Word List

(Conversation and Reading Practice)

backyard	garbage	milkman	straight
bowl	grass	note	supermarket
cut	hold	quart	upside down
dry cleaner	keep	refrigerator	why
eggs	laundry	secret	yolks
egg whites	love	shoe repairman	

UNIT 3 GETTING INFORMATION AND DIRECTIONS

331 Excuse me, sir. Can you give me some information?

332 Can you tell me where Peach Street is?

333 It's two blocks straight ahead.

334 Which direction is it to the theater?

335 Turn right at the next corner.

336 How far is it to the university?

337 It's a long way from here.

338 The school is just around the corner.

339 The restaurant is across the street from the hotel.

340 You can't miss it.

341 Do you happen to know Mr. Cooper's telephone number?

342 Could you tell me where the nearest telephone is?

343 Should I go this way, or that way?

344 Go that way for two blocks, then turn left.

345 I beg your pardon. Is this seat taken?

INTONATION

331   Excuse me, sir. Can you give me some information?

332   Can you tell me where Peach Street is?

333   It's two blocks straight ahead.

334   Which direction is it to the theater?

335   Turn right at the next corner.

336   How far is it to the university?

337   It's a long way from here.

338   The school is just around the corner.

339   The restaurant is across the street from the hotel.

340   You can't miss it.

341   Do you happen to know Mr. Cooper's telephone number?

342   Could you tell me where the nearest telephone is?

343   Should I go this way, or that way?

344   Go that way for two blocks, then turn left.

345   I beg your pardon. Is this seat taken?

VERB STUDY

1. **excuse**

   a. Excuse me, sir.
   b. The teacher excused me from class yesterday.
   c. The teacher excuses somebody from class every day.

2. **give**

   a. Can you give me some information?
   b. Mr. Cooper gave me a book.
   c. John gives me a newspaper every morning.

3. **turn**

   a. Turn right at the next corner.
   b. He turned right at the corner.
   c. Please turn the page.

4. **miss**

   a. You can't miss it.
   b. I didn't turn right, and I missed the street.
   c. I miss all my friends very much.
   d. He is in California now, and he misses his friends here in New York.

5. **go**

   a. Should I go this way, or that way?
   b. He goes this way, and I go that way.
   c. Yesterday I went to the restaurant at 6 p.m.
   d. I'm going to the restaurant tonight.

6. **beg**

   a. I beg your pardon.
   b. He begged my pardon.
   c. Every day he begs me to take several books home with me.

7. **happen to**

   a. Do you happen to know Mr. Cooper's telephone number?
   b. I just happened to know his telephone number.
   c. Yes, I know her. She happens to be my sister.
   d. Did you happen to listen to the radio last night?

SUBSTITUTION DRILLS

1. Excuse me,

| sir |
| miss |
| Officer |
| Captain |
| Colonel |

Can you give me some information?

2. Can you tell me where

| Peach Street |
| the restaurant |
| the post office |
| the airport |
| the railroad station |

is?

3. The post office is

| two blocks straight ahead |
| two miles straight ahead |
| on the other side of the street |

.

4. Which direction is it to

| the theater |
| the post office |
| the university |
| the bank |
| the church |

? Do you know?

5.

| Turn right |
| Turn left |
| Go straight ahead |
| Go to the right |
| Go to the left |

at the next corner. You can't miss it.

6. How far is it to the university?

| Can you tell me |
| Would you tell me |
| Could you tell me |
| Would you mind telling me |

?

7. It's a

| long way |
| short distance |
| short walk |
| long drive |

from here to the university.

8. The school is

| just around the corner |
| in the middle of the block |
| right on the corner |
| up there on the left |

. You can't miss it.

9. The restaurant is | across the street | from the hotel.
                     around the corner
                     a mile
                     a short walk

10. Do you happen to know Mr. Cooper's | telephone number | ?
                                     address
                                     profession
                                     age
                                     height and weight
                                     office address

11. I don't happen to know | his | address.
                          her
                          John's

12. Could you tell me where the nearest | telephone | is?
                                     hospital
                                     ladies' room
                                     men's room

13. Where's the | post office | ? Should I go this way, or that way?
                     university
                     bank
                     airport

14. Go that way for | two blocks | , then turn left.
                     a block or two
                     about two miles

15. I beg your pardon. Is this seat | taken | ?
                               occupied
                               reserved
                               reserved for somebody

16. The restaurant is | up those stairs | .
                     on the second floor
                     down those stairs
                     in the basement

17. Isn't the restaurant | straight ahead | ?
                       around the corner
                       in the middle of the next block
                       right on the corner of Washington Street

READING PRACTICE

Getting Information and Directions

Last week Bill had to go to New York. It was his first time there, and he didn't know his way around the city. He had a meeting at 10 o'clock, and he wanted to be on time. The meeting was in the Peterson Building on 34th Street, but Bill didn't know where that was. Seeing two men standing on a corner he asked them for directions.

"Pardon me," he said, "but can you tell me how to get to the Peterson Building on 34th Street?"

"Sure," answered one of the men. "You can get there in five minutes. Go to the next corner and turn left. Walk three blocks and there you are."

But the other man said: "There's a better way. Get on the bus here at this corner. It stops right near the Peters Building."

"Not Peters," Bill told him. "Peterson."

Then the first man said, "Oh, that's on *East* 34th Street, not *West* 34th. It's quite a distance from here. You'll have to take the subway."

But the second man told Bill: "No, don't go by subway. Take the crosstown bus. It goes to the Peterkin Building."

"Peterson. Not Peterkin." Bill looked at his watch. It was almost ten o'clock. "Thanks a lot," he said. "I think I'll take a taxi."

As he got into the taxi he saw the two men arguing and pointing in different directions. Next time he wanted to know how to get to a place, he'd ask a policeman!

Questions

1. Why did Bill have to go to New York?
2. What time was his meeting?
3. Who wanted to help Bill find the Peterson Building?
4. What did he finally do?
5. What did Bill want to do the next time he needed to ask directions?

CONVERSATION

1. Getting directions

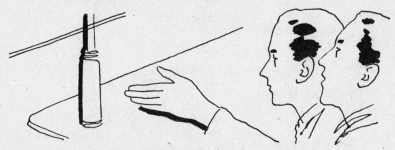

A: Excuse me. Can you tell me how to get to the post office?
B: Of course. It's very near here. Go to the corner and turn right. Walk one block and turn right again. Go across the street. The post office is on the corner. You can't miss it.
A: Thank you very much. I'm sure I'll find it.
B: There's one thing I forgot to tell you.
A: What's that?
B: Today is a holiday. The post office is closed.

2. Going to the movies

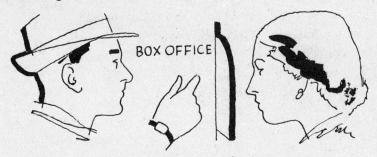

BOX OFFICE

A: What time does the complete show begin?
B: At seven o'clock. The first picture begins at seven-twenty.
A: How long does the complete program last?
B: The first show is finished at nine. The program lasts two hours.
A: Is the same picture on tomorrow night?
B: No. This is the last night.
A: Then I'll have to see it now. One ticket, please.

EXERCISES

1. Use the right word.

far	miss	right
across	long drive	miles
straight ahead	corner	
way	taken	

a. Which _____ is it to the post office?

b. Go _____ for three blocks.

c. How _____ is it to the hotel?

d. Turn left and you can't _____ it.

e. The theater is _____ the street.

f. The airport is a _____ from here.

g. The bank is five _____ from the church.

h. Excuse me, is this seat _____?

i. I should turn _____ at this corner.

j. The house is around the _____.

2. Student A asks the following questions. Student B gives complete answers, using the information given in parentheses.

Example: Student A: Where are you going?
Student B: (home) I'm going home.

a. A: Where is Peach Street?
B: (two miles straight ahead)

b. A: How far is the bank?
B: (five miles from here)

c. A: Where is the nearest restaurant?
B: (across the street)

d. A: Which direction should I go to get to the post office?
B: (to the right at the next corner)

e. A: Could you tell me where the nearest telephone is?
B: (in the men's room or in the ladies' room)

f. A: Would you mind telling me where the school is?
B: (in the middle of the next block)

g. A: Do you happen to know where the railroad station is?
B: (*around the corner*)

h. A: Would you tell me where the National Theater is?
B: (*right on the corner of Washington Street*)

i. A: How far is it from here to the airport?
B: (*a long drive*)

j. A: Which direction is it to the university?
B: (*about two miles to the left*)

3. Change the following sentences to questions beginning with the question words given.

Examples: *He* is a student. Who *is a student?*
He's going *to the university.* Where *is he going?*

a. The church is *a long way* from here. How far _____?

b. The bank is *across the street.* Where _____?

c. This seat is reserved for *Mr. Cooper.* Who _____?

d. I don't know my *neighbor's* address. Whose _____?

e. We should turn *right* at the next corner. Which way _____?

f. *The restaurant* is a short walk from the hotel. What _____?

g. *The school* is around the corner. What _____?

h. *The officer* gave me some information. Who _____?

i. The National Theater is *straight ahead.* Which way _____?

j. The telephone is *in the basement.* Where _____?

k. The post office will open *at 8 a.m.* What time _____?

l. Mr. Cooper is *sixty-one years old.* How old _____?

m. The airport is *ten miles* from the town. How far _____?

n. I'm going to school *this afternoon.* When _____?

o. This table is reserved for Mr. Cooper *every day.* How often _____?

p. This is *John's* telephone number. Whose _____?

q. *The seat near the window* is occupied. Which seat _____?

WORD LIST

across	drive	railroad
airport	height	reserved
around	information	seat
bank	ladies' room	sir
basement	men's room	stairs
captain	miss	station
church	number	straight ahead
colonel	occupied	up
corner	officer	walk
direction	post office	way
down	profession	

Verb Forms

happen to, happened to (*p. and p. part.*)
miss, missed (*p. and p. part.*)
turn, turned (*p. and p. part.*)

Expressions

be taken
I beg your pardon

Supplementary Word List

(Conversation and Reading Practice)

better	east	policeman
building	find	subway
bus	holiday	ticket
complete	last	west
crosstown	pointing	

UNIT 4 TALKING ABOUT FAMILY AND RELATIVES

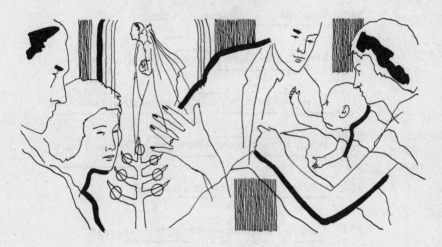

346 Are you married?

347 No, I'm not married. I'm still single.

348 Your niece is engaged, isn't she?

349 My sister has been engaged for two months.

350 My grandfather got married in 1921.

351 When is your grandparents' wedding anniversary?

352 How long have they been married?

353 They've been married for quite a few years.

354 Who did George marry?

355 Do they have children?

356 They had a baby last month.

357 My son wants to get married in June.

358 They don't know when the wedding will be.

359 Their grandchildren are grown up now.

360 She's a widow. Her husband died last year.

INTONATION

346   Are you married?

347   No, I'm not married. I'm still single.

348   Your niece is engaged, isn't she?

349   My sister has been engaged for two months.

350   My grandfather got married in nineteen twenty-one.

351   When is your grandparents' wedding anniversary?

352. How long have they been married?

353   They've been married for quite a few years.

354   Who did George marry?

355   Do they have children?

356   They had a baby last month.

357   My son wants to get married in June.

358   They don't know when the wedding will be.

359   Their grandchildren are grown up now.

360   She's a widow. Her husband died last year.

VERB STUDY

1. **marry**

   a. Who did George marry?
   b. George married Elizabeth.
   c. He married her last year.

2. **be married**

   a. Are you married?
   b. No, I'm not married.
   c. My brother isn't married either.
   d. Was he married in California?

3. **get married**

   a. My grandfather got married in 1921.
   b. My son wants to get married in June.
   c. She's getting married tonight.

4. **be engaged (have been engaged)**

   a. Your niece is engaged, isn't she?
   b. I'm engaged.
   c. When I met her, she was engaged.
   d. My sister has been engaged for two months.
   e. How long have they been engaged?

5. **want to**

   a. My son wants to get married in June.
   b. Does she want to get married this year?
   c. I wanted to have breakfast at 6 o'clock this morning.
   d. We want to go home now.

6. **die**

   a. Her husband died last year.
   b. Did his cousin die last July?
   c. His grandfather died in California.

SUBSTITUTION DRILLS

1. My cousin is | still single | .
   a bachelor
   an only child

2. Your niece is | engaged | , isn't she?
   married

3. My sister has been | engaged | for two months.
   married

4. My | grandfather | got married in 1945.
   grandmother
   grandson
   granddaughter

5. | How long | have they been married?
   Approximately how long
   How many years
   Exactly how many years

6. I'm single, and my | cousin | is still single.
   uncle
   nephew
   brother

7. Is your | niece | married?
   aunt
   cousin
   sister

8. When did your | cousin | get married? Was it last year?
   uncle
   aunt
   friend

9. Who did | George | marry?
   you
   she
   your cousin
   Mr. Cooper

10. Do Mr. and Mrs. Cooper have

children
any children
several children
a child

?

11. They had

a baby
a child
another child

last month, didn't they?

12.

My son
My daughter
His brother
Our grandchild
Their cousin

wants to get married in June.

13. Their grandchildren are

grown up
married
engaged

now, aren't they?

14. She's a widow. Her husband

died
passed away

last year.

15.

I'm
He's
She's
They're

not married.

16. They don't know when the wedding

will be
is going to be
is supposed to be
will take place

.

17. They've been married for

quite a few years
many years
quite a long time
years and years

.

18. When is your

grandparents'
parents'
friends'
brother's

wedding anniversary?

READING PRACTICE

Talking About Family and Relatives

A golden wedding anniversary is a celebration of fifty years of marriage. Usually there is a big party for all the friends and relatives of the married couple. Just think what a lot of people this can be! There are sons and daughters, nieces and nephews, brothers and sisters, cousins, grandchildren—even great-grandchildren. Of course many old friends come, too.

Frequently, members of the family from different towns don't see each other very often. They are glad to come to an anniversary party.

But it can be a time of confusion for the children. It's hard for them to remember the names of all their relatives. "Albert," one mother will say, "this is your cousin George. He's really your second cousin because he's Dorothy's son. Dorothy is my first cousin. Her mother is Aunt Helen, my father's sister."

At times there are stepsisters, half-brothers and nieces-in-law. There are "aunts" and "uncles" who aren't relatives at all, but good friends of the family! It can be very confusing, but everyone has a good time.

Questions

1. What is a golden wedding anniversary?
2. Have you ever been to this kind of celebration?
3. What do we call the children of grandchildren?
4. Name four types of relatives.
5. How many cousins do you have? Do you know them all by name?

CONVERSATION

Meeting relatives

JEAN: I just got a letter from Aunt Caroline. You remember her, don't you, David? My great-aunt. Grandma Allen's sister.

DAVID: Yes, I remember. She's the one who has been married twice. Her first husband died, didn't he?

JEAN: That's right. And she has children from each marriage. Uncle Jim, her second husband, was married before, too. He has four children from his first marriage. He and Aunt Caroline have three.

DAVID: Then they are all your cousins, aren't they?

JEAN: I call them all cousin. All of Aunt Caroline's children are my first cousins, but Uncle Jim's children from his first marriage are not relatives of mine.

DAVID: What are they to each other?

JEAN: Let's see. Aunt Caroline's sons and daughters from her first marriage are Uncle Jim's stepchildren. Aunt Caroline is his children's stepmother. The children are stepbrothers and stepsisters.

DAVID: I've never understood that. I thought they were half-brothers and half-sisters.

JEAN: No. Half-brothers and half-sisters have the same mother or the same father. Aunt Caroline's and Uncle Jim's children are half-brothers and half-sisters to the other children.

DAVID: It's very confusing. But what does Aunt Caroline say in her letter?

JEAN: They're all coming to visit us next week.

DAVID: What? I'll never know who is who!

EXERCISES

1. Complete the sentences with the appropriate word from the list.

grandparents	aunt	uncle
cousin	grandchildren	niece
nephew	brother	sister
grandmother	grandfather	husband

    a. My father's parents are my _____.

    b. My mother's sister is my _____.

    c. My mother's brother is my _____.

    d. My uncle's son is my _____.

    e. My sister's daughter is my _____.

    f. My brother's son is my _____.

    g. My son's children are my _____.

    h. My uncle is my father's _____.

    i. My aunt is my father's _____.

    j. My father's mother is my _____.

    k. My father's father is my _____.

    l. My father is my mother's _____.

2. Use the possessive form of the pronoun in each of the following sentences.

    Example: *My* brother had another child. (*I*)

    a. _____ children want to get married. (*We*)

    b. _____ cousin has been married for a long time. (*I*)

    c. When is _____ grandparents' wedding anniversary? (*you*)

    d. _____ grandchildren are grown up now. (*They*)

    e. _____ wedding will take place in June. (*He*)

    f. _____ husband passed away last year. (*She*)

3. Use contractions whenever possible in each sentence.

   Example: I am not married. *I'm not married.*

   a. She is a widow. Her husband died last year.
   b. He is engaged to be married.
   c. They are going to have a baby.
   d. You are still single.
   e. They do not know when the wedding will be.
   f. She did not get married last year.
   g. Mr. and Mrs. Cooper do not have any children, but they would like to.
   h. George is not a bachelor; he has been married for a long time.
   i. I am a bachelor, but I would like to get married.
   j. They have been married for approximately three years.
   k. I am going to get married in exactly three days.
   l. My sister has been engaged for two months.
   m. Today is my parents' anniversary.

4. Attach a tag question to each of the following sentences as shown in the examples.

   Examples: He wants to study, *doesn't he?*
               He's going to school, *isn't he?*

   a. Your nephew is engaged.
   b. Your granddaughter got married in 1945.
   c. You're still a bachelor.
   d. They had a child last month.
   e. Yesterday was your anniversary.
   f. They've been married for many years.
   g. She's been a widow since last year.
   h. Mr. and Mrs. Cooper have several children.
   i. Your wedding will take place in June.
   j. You're engaged now.
   k. Your niece is married.
   l. You got married last year.

WORD LIST

anniversary	granddaughter	married
approximately	grandfather	nephew
baby	grandmother	niece
bachelor	grandparent	single
engaged	grandson	wedding
grandchild, grandchildren	grown up	widow

Verb Forms

die, died (*p. and p. part.*)
marry, married (*p. and p. part.*)
pass away, passed away
   (*p. and p. part.*)
take place, took place (*p.*),
   taken place (*p. part.*)

Expressions

be supposed to
get married

Supplementary Word List
(Conversation and Reading Practice)

because	great-aunt	nieces-in-law
call	great-grandchildren	stepbrothers
celebration	half-brothers	stepchildren
confusing	half-sisters	stepmother
confusion	marriage	stepsisters
golden	members	

UNIT 5 TALKING ABOUT NEIGHBORS AND FRIENDS

361   Where did you grow up?

362   I grew up right here in this neighborhood.

363   My friend spent his childhood in California.

364   He lived in California until he was seventeen.

365   There have been a lot of changes here in the last 20 years.

366   There used to be a grocery store on the corner.

367   All of those houses have been built in the last ten years.

368   They're building a new house up the street from me.

369   If you buy that home, will you spend the rest of your life there?

370   Are your neighbors very friendly?

371   We all know each other pretty well.

372   A young married couple moved in next door to us.

373   Who bought that new house down the street from you?

374   An elderly man rented the big white house.

375   What beautiful trees those are!

INTONATION

361 Where did you grow up?

362 I grew up right here in this neighborhood.

363 My friend spent his childhood in California.

364 He lived in California until he was seventeen.

365 There have been a lot of changes here in the last 20 years.

366 There used to be a grocery store on the corner.

367 All of those houses have been built in the last ten years.

368 They're building a new house up the street from me.

369 If you buy that home, will you spend the rest of your life there?

370 Are your neighbors very friendly?

371 We all know each other pretty well.

372 A young married couple moved in next door to us.

373 Who bought that new house down the street from you?

374 An elderly man rented the big white house.

375 What beautiful trees those are!

VERB STUDY

1. **grow up**

   a. Where did you grow up?
   b. I grew up here in this neighborhood.
   c. I've grown up here in this city.

2. **spend (one's) childhood**

   a. My friend spent his childhood in California.
   b. Where did you spend your childhood?

3. **build (be building)**

   a. They built a new house.
   b. They're building a new house up the street from me.
   c. Are you building a new house this year?

4. **be built (have been built)**

   a. Those houses were built last year.
   b. All of those houses have been built in the last 10 years.
   c. When were those houses built?

5. **move in (be moving in)**

   a. A young married couple moved in next door.
   b. When did they move in?
   c. You moved in yesterday, didn't you?
   d. They're moving in today.

6. **buy**

   a. Who bought that house?
   b. If you buy that house, will you live there several years?
   c. If he buys that house, will he live there several years?

7. **know (each other)**

   a. We all know each other pretty well.
   b. Do they know each other very well?
   c. Did they know each other last year?
   d. We knew each other in California several years ago.

8. **there has been, there have been**

   a. There have been many changes in the last 20 years.
   b. There has been a change in John in the last few days.
   c. Have there been many changes here in the last five years?

SUBSTITUTION DRILLS

1. Where did
   | you |
   | she |
   | he |
   | Peter and John |
   | they |
   grow up?

2. I grew up
   | in this neighborhood |
   | in this city |
   | on a farm |
   | in a little country town |
   . Where did you grow up?

3. My friend spent his
   | childhood |
   | early childhood |
   | early years |
   | childhood years |
   in California.

4. He lived in
   | California |
   | Texas |
   | New York |
   | Virginia |
   until he was seventeen.

5. There have been a lot of
   | changes |
   | developments |
   | improvements |
   here in the last 20 years.

6. There used to be a
   | grocery store |
   | drugstore |
   | department store |
   | movie theater |
   on the corner.

7.
   | All |
   | Some |
   | A few |
   | Many |
   | Almost all |
   of those houses have been built in the last 10 years.

8. They're building a new
   | house |
   | apartment house |
   | building |
   | office building |
   up the street from me.

9. If you | buy | that home, will you spend the rest of your life
       | purchase | there?
       | rent |

10. Are your neighbors very | friendly | ?
       | kind |
       | quiet |
       | noisy |

11. | We all | know each other pretty well.
    | Some of us |
    | A few of us |
    | Most of us |
    | Three or four of us |

12. A young married couple | moved in | next door to us.
       | has moved in |
       | is moving in |
       | is going to move in |

13. Who bought that new house | down the street | from you?
       | up the street |
       | across the street |
       | around the corner |
       | two blocks |

14. An elderly man | rented | the big white house.
       | has rented |
       | is renting |
       | is going to rent |

15. What beautiful | trees | those are!
       | flowers |
       | homes |
       | trees and flowers |

16. We all | know each other pretty well | . We're neighbors.
       | see each other often |
       | talk to each other every day |
       | help each other all the time |

READING PRACTICE

Talking About Neighbors and Friends

Last summer, my wife Jane and I went to visit the town where we both grew up. We hadn't been there since we were married ten years ago.

First, we went to the neighborhood where my wife spent her childhood. It hadn't changed very much. The house where she was born was still there, but it was now a different color. The same neighbors still lived next door. They were very glad to see Jane, and asked us to come in and have a cup of coffee. We learned about all the neighbors, old and new. Jane had a very good time. As fast as one question was answered, she would ask the next. "What happened to the Dunbars who used to have the little yellow house on the corner?" "Who bought the old Johnson place in the next block?" "Do Fred and Martha Alberts still live down the street?" "What about Miss Burton who lived alone in that extremely big house around the corner?"

Then we went to see the neighborhood where I grew up. What a disappointment! It was all changed. All the old houses I remembered were gone and in their place were some very modern ones. I didn't know any of the people who lived there.

Someone has said that you can't go home again. Jane might not think so, but I believe this is true.

Questions

1. How long had it been since Jane and her husband visited their hometown?
2. Had Jane's neighborhood changed very much?
3. How did she learn all the news about her neighborhood?
4. Was Jane's husband's neighborhood the same as when he lived there?
5. Is it true that "you can't go home again"?

CONVERSATION

1. Looking for a new house

SALESMAN: I think I have exactly the house you are looking for, Mr. James. It's in a very good neighborhood.

MR. JAMES: Fine. Is it near a shopping center?

SALESMAN: Yes, it is. The shopping center is just a short walk. And the school, too.

MR. JAMES: Good. Is the house very old? I'd like a new one.

SALESMAN: All the houses here are very modern. None of them are over five years old.

MR. JAMES: I'd like to see the house. From what you tell me it is just what I want.

SALESMAN: I can take you to see it now.

2. Neighborhood friends

MABEL: Have you met our new neighbors yet? They moved in last Saturday.

KITTY: No, I haven't. I understand they are renting the house. They aren't buying it.

MABEL: That's right. I've talked to one of the children. He's the same age as my son. There are five in the family: the parents, two sons, and a daughter.

KITTY: Let's go and welcome the new family to the neighborhood. I'm sure they'd like that.

MABEL: That's a good idea. Perhaps there is something we can do for them.

KITTY: Everyone was very kind when I moved here two years ago. It's good to feel welcome in a new neighborhood.

EXERCISES

1. Use the right form of "grow up."
   Example: I *grew up* in Texas.

   a. Children _____ fast.

   b. John _____ in California.

   c. Where did they _____?

   d. They _____ in New York.

   e. Boys _____ to be men.

   f. A girl _____ to be a woman.

2. Use the right form of "wake up."
   Example: I *wake up* at 7 o'clock every day.

   a. Yesterday morning I _____ at ten o'clock.

   b. I usually _____ at eight.

   c. My family often _____ before 6:30.

   d. My brother _____ on time this morning.

   e. Last night they _____ at midnight.

3. Use the right form of "spend."
   Example: I *spend* every day at work.

   a. John _____ his childhood in New York.

   b. Will you _____ the night at my house?

   c. Yes, I'll _____ the night.

   d. I _____ last week in California.

   e. My sister _____ her childhood in Texas.

4. Complete the sentences with the correct word from the list.

on	up
from	until
of	in

   a. There have been a lot _____ improvements here.

b. I grew _____ in a small country town.

c. There used to be a grocery store _____ the corner.

d. A young married couple moved _____ next door.

e. We bought the new house two blocks _____ you.

f. He lived in Texas _____ he was seventeen.

g. An elderly man rented the house _____ us.

h. I spent my childhood _____ a farm.

i. Many of those houses have been built _____ the last ten years.

j. The movie theater is _____ the street from me.

5. Change the following sentences to exclamations as shown in the examples.

> Examples: That tree is large.
> *What a large tree that is!*
>
> Those are beautiful trees.
> *What beautiful trees those are!*

a. That is a large building.
b. Those flowers are beautiful.
c. You have quiet neighbors.
d. He had a happy childhood.
e. This neighborhood is noisy.
f. That couple is friendly.

6. Answer the following questions. Give short answers as shown in the example.

Example: Do you live in Virginia? *Yes, I do.*

a. Did Peter grow up on a farm? Yes, _____.

b. Did you spend your childhood in California? Yes, _____.

c. Has an elderly woman rented that new house? Yes, _____.

d. Do you know that couple next door? No, _____.

e. Are you building a new house next month? Yes, _____.

f. Has Mr. Jones bought that office building yet? No, _____.

g. Will Mrs. Jones buy a new house? No, _____.

h. Did Mary know Mrs. Jones last month? Yes, _____.

i. Have there been a lot of improvements in this neighborhood? Yes, _____.

j. Are those neighbors very friendly? Yes, _____.

WORD LIST

beautiful	each other	kind
building	elderly	new
change	farm	noisy
childhood	flower	quiet
couple	friendly	the rest of
department store	grocery store	tree
development	improvement	until
drugstore		

Verb Forms

buy, bought (*p. and p. part.*)
build, built (*p. and p. part.*)
grow up, grew up (*p.*),
   grown up (*p. part.*)
move in, moved in (*p. and p. part.*)
purchase, purchased
   (*p. and p. part.*)
rent, rented (*p. and p. part.*)
spend, spent (*p. and p. part.*)

Expressions

all the time
know (someone)
spend (one's) childhood

Supplementary Word List

(Conversation and Reading Practice)

again	modern
alone	shopping center
changed	true
disappointment	welcome
idea	

REVIEW ONE

1. Conversation Review and Practice

a. Weighing things

A: How much does that book weigh?

B: I don't know. Let's weigh it.

A: It weighs nearly two pounds.

B: This dark blue book weighs just as much as that green book.

A: How much does that table weigh? Can you tell me?

B: It's not awfully heavy, but I don't know the exact weight.

A: It must weigh about forty or fifty pounds.

B: I'd say it weighs nearly seventy pounds.

A: Can you tell me how much that typewriter weighs?

B: No, I can't. I don't know what the weight of the typewriter is.

A: How much do you weigh?

B: I don't know how much I weigh. Maybe I weigh about two hundred pounds.

A: Does your brother know his exact weight?

B: No, he doesn't. He doesn't know how much he weighs.

b. Measuring things

A: Will you please measure that window to see how wide it is?

B: It's twenty-eight inches wide.

A: How high is that window? Will you measure it?

B: It's not very high. It's forty-one inches in height.

A: This window is just as wide as that one, isn't it?

B: Yes, it is. But this window is higher than that one.

A: What's the width of those walls?

B: These walls are exactly two inches thick.

A: How wide is Jones Boulevard? Do you know?

B: I'd say it's about seventy-five feet wide.

A: Jones Boulevard is wider than Baltimore Avenue, isn't it?

B: Yes, it is. Baltimore Avenue is only fifty feet wide.

c. Asking for help

A: Will you please do me a favor?
B: Yes. What can I do?

A: Please bring me those magazines.
B: Here they are. They're not very heavy.

A: Now, would you help me move this heavy box?
B: Yes. Oh, this box is very heavy!

A: Yes, it is. Now, I have to wrap the box.
B: Let's put the box down on the table.

A: Fine. Get me a yardstick from the kitchen, will you?
B: Yes. What color is the yardstick?

A: The yardstick is yellow. And get me a hammer,too, will you?
B: Yes, I will. Here you are.

A: Would you mind mailing this package for me this afternoon?
B: I can't. I won't have time to mail the package.

d. Getting help

A: Would you please tell Mr. Cooper that I'm here?
B: Mr. Cooper is very busy right now.

A: Would you please ask him to call me tomorrow?
B: I'll ask him to call you.

A: Please bring me my coat. I hung it up in the closet.
B: Here's your coat. Is this your hat, too?

A: Yes, it is. Put my hat down on the table, will you please?
B: Yes. Would you mind doing a favor for me?

A: What can I do for you?
B: Would you mind mailing this letter for me?

A: I'll mail the letter for you. I'm not very busy today.
B: Thank you very much. If you're able to, please mail this package, too.

2. Review Exercises

Use the proper verb form.

a. How much does this typewriter _____? (*weigh*)

b. I _____ the suitcase this morning. (*weigh*)

c. I _____ last night's movie very much. (*like*)

d. This material _____ soft, doesn't it? (*feel*)

e. Last year Mr. Cooper _____ a good automobile. (*own*)

f. Does he _____ a dark blue book? (*have*)

g. My friend _____ the window to see how wide it was. (*measure*)

h. I don't know the weight of that book, but this one _____ two pounds. (*weigh*)

i. I already _____ John to help you. (*ask*)

j. Is he _____ you? (*bother*)

k. He _____ my coat in the closet an hour ago. (*hang up*)

l. Would you mind _____ this package? (*wrap*)

m. Would you do me the favor of _____ this milk into that glass? (*pour*)

n. They're _____ a new house up the street from me. (*build*)

o. You _____ yesterday, didn't you? (*move in*)

p. My friend _____ his childhood in California. (*spend*)

q. If he _____ that house, will he live there several years? (*buy*)

r. There _____ be a department store on the corner. (*use to*)

s. I _____ in a little country town not far from here. (*grow up*)

t. Who _____ that new house down the street from you? (*buy*)

u. What beautiful homes these _____! (*be*)

v. Would you mind _____ me how far it is to the university? (*tell*)

w. Could you tell me where the nearest telephone _____? (*be*)

x. My grandfather _____ in 1931. (*get married*)

y. Her husband _____ last year. (*die*)

z. My daughter _____ get married next June. (*want to*)

3. Answer the questions

    a. What size suitcase do you own?

    b. What street do you live on?

    c. What's your address?

    d. Do you know where Jones Boulevard is?

    e. Have you ever measured a window to see how wide it was?

    f. How much does a typewriter weigh?

    g. Do you write many letters?

    h. Do you happen to know Mr. Cooper's telephone number?

    i. By the way, who is Mr. Cooper? Do you know him?

    j. Are you married?

    k. Do you know when your grandfather got married?

    l. Where did you grow up?

    m. Are your neighbors very friendly?

4. Conversation Practice

You are looking for Peach Street and the university, and a man gives you directions.

First you ask for information.
> You:
> The man:

You want to find Peach Street, and the man tells you where to go.
> You:
> The man:

Then you ask the man where the university is, and he tells you.

      — — —

You thank the man and say good-bye to him.

      — — —

5. Review Sentences

Study and review Base Sentences 301 to 375.

UNIT 6 TALKING ABOUT FUTURE ACTIVITIES

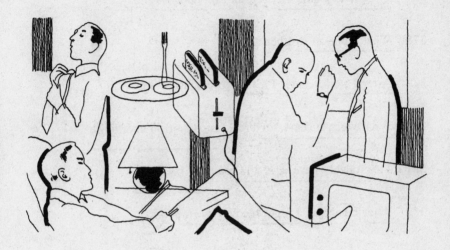

376 What time are you going to get up tomorrow morning?

377 I'll probably wake up early and get up at 6:30.

378 What will you do then?

379 After I get dressed, I'll have breakfast.

380 What will you have for breakfast tomorrow morning?

381 I'll probably have eggs and toast for breakfast.

382 After breakfast, I'll get ready to go to work.

383 I'll leave the house at 8:00 and get to the office at 8:30.

384 I'll probably go out for lunch at about 12:30.

385 I'll finish working at 5:30 and get home by 6 o'clock.

386 Are you going to have dinner at home tomorrow night?

387 Do you think you'll go to the movies tomorrow night?

388 I'll probably stay home and watch television.

389 When I get sleepy, I'll probably get ready for bed.

390 Do you think you'll be able to go to sleep right away?

INTONATION

376 What time are you going to get up tomorrow morning?

377 I'll probably wake up early and get up at six thirty.

378 What will you do then?

379 After I get dressed, I'll have breakfast.

380 What will you have for breakfast tomorrow morning?

381 I'll probably have eggs and toast for breakfast.

382 After breakfast, I'll get ready to go to work.

383 I'll leave the house at eight and get to the office at eight thirty.

384 I'll probably go out for lunch at about twelve thirty.

385 I'll finish working at five thirty, and get home by six o'clock.

386 Are you going to have dinner at home tomorrow night?

387 Do you think you'll go to the movies tomorrow night?

388 I'll probably stay home and watch television.

389 When I get sleepy, I'll probably get ready for bed.

390 Do you think you'll be able to go to sleep right away?

VERB STUDY

1. **get up**
   a. What time are you going to get up tomorrow?
   b. I got up at 6 o'clock yesterday.
   c. She gets up at 7:30 every day.
   d. I'm getting up right now.

2. **wake up, go to sleep**
   a. I'll probably wake up early tomorrow.
   b. I woke up at 6 o'clock yesterday morning.
   c. My brother wakes up at 9 o'clock every day.
   d. Do you think you'll be able to go to sleep right away?
   e. He goes to sleep at 11:30 every night.

3. **get dressed**
   a. I get dressed at 9 o'clock every day.
   b. He got dressed at 8 o'clock yesterday morning.
   c. She gets dressed at 7 o'clock every day.
   d. Did you get dressed before breakfast this morning?

4. **stay**
   a. I'll probably stay home tonight.
   b. He stays home every night.
   c. She stayed home last night.

5. **watch**
   a. I watch television after dinner every night.
   b. He watches television after breakfast each day.
   c. We watched television last night until midnight.
   d. Did you watch television last Sunday?

6. **do**
   a. What will you do then?
   b. What are you doing now?
   c. She does the same thing every day.

7. **leave**
   a. I'll leave the house at 8 o'clock tomorrow.
   b. He left the house at 9 o'clock yesterday morning.
   c. She leaves the house at 10 o'clock every day.

8. **be able to**
   a. Do you think you'll be able to sleep immediately?
   b. I'm always able to go to sleep immediately.
   c. Were you able to talk with Mr. Cooper yesterday?

SUBSTITUTION DRILLS

1. What time | are | you / we / they | going to get up tomorrow morning?
           | is | she / he

2. I'll / We'll / You'll / They'll / She'll / He'll   probably wake up early tomorrow morning.

3. What will you do | then / at that time / after that / next | ? Will you get dressed?

4. After | I / you | get | dressed, it will be time for breakfast.
        | she / he | gets

5. After John gets dressed, he'll | have breakfast / go to work / leave the house to go to work / read the newspaper .

6. What | will you / are you going to / do you think you'll | have for breakfast tomorrow morning?

7. After breakfast, I'll get ready to | go to work / leave the house / write some letters .

8. I'll leave / I'm going to leave / Every day I leave / Yesterday I left / I used to leave   the house at 8 o'clock.

9. He'll get | home by 6 o'clock.
   He's going to get
   Every day he gets
   Yesterday he got
   He used to get

10. I'll finish | working | at 5:30.
    eating dinner
    writing letters
    reading the newspaper

11. Do you think | you'll go | to the movies tomorrow
    John will go | night?
    Peter and John will go

12. Do you think | you'll | be able to go to sleep right away?
    John will
    your friend will

13. What time are you going to get up | tomorrow morning | ?
    the day after tomorrow
    next Tuesday morning
    a week from Saturday
    morning

14. I'll be able to go to sleep | right away | .
    immediately

15. Will Mr. Cooper be able to | have breakfast | with us?
    go out for lunch
    eat dinner
    watch television
    speak French

16. Do you think you'll go to the movies | tomorrow night | ?
    Saturday night
    next week
    next weekend
    a week from today

17. John will probably wake up | early tomorrow morning | .
    late this afternoon
    in the middle of the night
    at the crack of dawn

READING PRACTICE

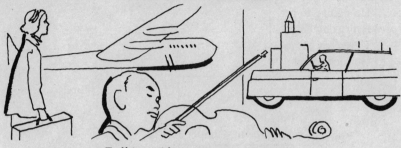

Talking About Future Activities

Marie works hard in an office all week. On Saturday and Sunday she has a very busy social life. This weekend she's going to Boston. She has never been there and she wants to see as much as she can while she is there. This is Marie's plan:

When she finishes work on Friday afternoon, she'll take a taxi to the airport and fly to Boston. She'll go to her hotel and leave her suitcase there. Then she'll have dinner with some friends who live in Boston.

Marie's friends know Boston very well. They are going to take her to all the interesting places. Friday evening after dinner they are going to drive around the city in their car. That way Marie will be able to see Boston at night.

On Saturday morning Marie will get up early. After she has breakfast, her friends are going to drive her to the historic towns of Concord and Lexington. They will have lunch at a restaurant in Concord. Then they will visit Harvard University, which is in Cambridge, across the river from Boston. By that time it will be evening. Marie and her friends are going to go to a concert by the Boston Symphony Orchestra. There will be two symphonies by Beethoven on the program.

On Sunday, after visiting other interesting parts of the city, Marie will go to the airport and fly home. She knows she will have a good time in Boston. She'll probably want to visit it again some day.

Questions

1. Where is Marie going for the weekend? Has she been there before?
2. When is she leaving? How will she go to Boston?
3. What are Marie's plans for Friday evening?
4. Where will she go on Saturday?
5. Does Marie have any plans for Saturday evening? What are they?
6. Have you ever been to Boston?

CONVERSATION

Detectives at work

DETECTIVE A: We don't have much time, so listen to me. I'll tell you what we are going to do.

DETECTIVE B: I'll write it down while you're talking.

A: The man we want does everything at exactly the same time every evening. I've watched him for three days.

B: You don't think he'll change his plan tonight, do you?

A: I'm sure he won't. At 7 o'clock he'll come down those stairs and go into the restaurant next door.

B: Are you sure he'll eat in that restaurant and not in another one?

A: He'll eat in that one. He'll get a steak, a baked potato, and a tossed green salad.

B: Where will he sit?

A: He'll take the first table by the window. And he'll look out at the street.

B: We'll have to be careful when we go into the restaurant to get him.

A: We won't go into the restaurant. We don't want him to see us.

B: What will we do?

A: We'll wait for him in the street. We'll get him when he finishes eating and leaves the restaurant.

B: Look! There he is now. Let's go.

EXERCISES

1. Complete the sentences with the correct form of the verb in parentheses.

   Examples: Yesterday I *went* to school. (*go*)

   I *go* to school every day. (*go*)

   I *will go* to school tomorrow. (*go*)

   a. Yesterday I _____ the house at 8:00. (*leave*)

   b. I _____ the house at 8:00 every day. (*leave*)

   c. I _____ the house at 8:00 tomorrow. (*leave*)

   d. I _____ to work last week. (*go*)

   e. I _____ to work today. (*go*)

   f. I _____ to work tomorrow morning. (*go*)

   g. I _____ late yesterday. (*be*)

   h. If I don't hurry, I _____ late today. (*be*)

   i. John _____ in the middle of last night. (*wake up*)

   j. John _____ at the crack of dawn tomorrow. (*wake up*)

   k. I _____ television last Saturday. (*watch*)

   l. I _____ television next Tuesday morning. (*watch*)

2. Use contractions wherever possible in the following sentences.

   Examples: I will go to school tonight. *I'll go to school tonight.*

   I will not go to school tonight.

   I won't go to school tonight.

   a. John will probably wake up soon.

   b. He will have breakfast after he wakes up.

   c. Then he will get ready to go to work.

   d. After that he will leave the house.

e. He will read the newspaper on the way to work.

f. John will not wake up in the middle of the night.

g. He will not go out for breakfast.

h. He will not leave the house before breakfast.

i. He will not finish working until 5:30.

j. He will not get home by 6:30.

k. He will get home at 7:00.

l. He will be able to eat dinner with us.

m. Next he will probably watch television.

n. After that he will go to sleep.

3. Change each of the following to a question beginning "Do you think . . . ?" Follow the examples. Use contractions wherever possible.

Examples: Will John go to school tonight?
Do you think John'll go to school tonight?

Did he go to school last night?
Do you think he went to school last night?

a. Will you finish reading the newspaper at 5:30?

b. Did he get home by 6:00 yesterday?

c. Will John go to the movies with us?

d. Will she be able to go out for lunch?

e. Did they wake up early yesterday morning?

f. Did he use to leave the house at 8 o'clock?

g. Will you be able to make some phone calls after breakfast?

h. Did they write some letters after breakfast?

i. Will we finish working at 5:30?

j. Will I be able to get home by 6 o'clock?

k. Did your friend go to sleep right away?

l. Did John make some phone calls early this morning?

m. Will she be ready to go to work right away?

n. Will Mr. Cooper be able to eat dinner with us a week from today?

WORD LIST

egg
probably
weekend

Verb Forms	Expressions
stay, stayed (*p. and p. part.*)	crack of dawn
	get ready
	get sleepy

Supplementary Word List

(Conversation and Reading Practice)

baked potato	drive	social
careful	fly	steak
change	historic	symphonies
concert	plan	tossed salad
detectives	river	

UNIT 7 TALKING ABOUT THE WEATHER

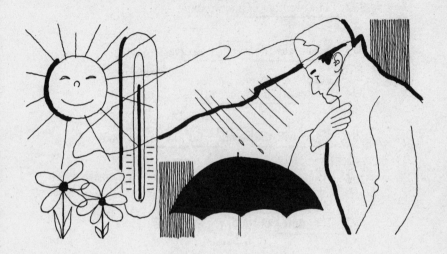

391 How is the weather today?

392 The weather is nice today.

393 What was the weather like yesterday?

394 Yesterday it rained all day.

395 What will the weather be like tomorrow?

396 It's going to snow tomorrow.

397 It's quite cold today.

398 It's been cloudy all morning.

399 Is it raining now?

400 It'll probably clear up this afternoon.

401 The days are getting hotter.

402 Today is the first day of spring.

403 What's the temperature today?

404 It's about seventy degrees Fahrenheit this afternoon.

405 There's a cool breeze this evening.

INTONATION

391   How is the weather today?

392   The weather is nice today.

393   What was the weather like yesterday?

394   Yesterday it rained all day.

395   What will the weather be like tomorrow?

396   It's going to snow tomorrow.

397   It's quite cold today.

398   It's been cloudy all morning.

399   Is it raining now?

400   It'll probably clear up this afternoon.

401   The days are getting hotter.

402   Today is the first day of spring.

403   What's the temperature today?

404   It's about seventy degrees Fahrenheit this afternoon.

405   There's a cool breeze this evening.

VERB STUDY

1. **rain**

   a. Yesterday it rained all day.
   b. Is it raining now?
   c. Do you think it will rain tomorrow?
   d. How hard did it rain last night?

2. **snow**

   a. It's going to snow tomorrow.
   b. It snowed all day yesterday, didn't it?
   c. Is it snowing now?

3. **clear up**

   a. It'll probably clear up this afternoon.
   b. It cleared up at about 3 o'clock yesterday afternoon.
   c. It clears up every day before 12 o'clock noon.
   d. It's clearing up now, isn't it?
   e. Has it cleared up yet?

4. **get (hotter), be getting (hotter)**

   a. The days are getting hotter.
   b. The days get hotter every week.
   c. Are the days getting much hotter?
   d. The days have gotten hotter, haven't they?

5. **have been**

   a. It's been cloudy all morning.
   b. Has it been cloudy all morning?
   c. I have been very well, thank you.
   d. Has she ever been in California?

6. **be like**

   a. What will the weather be like tomorrow?
   b. What was it like yesterday?
   c. The weather is nice today. It's just like a spring day.
   d. What is the weather like in Florida?

SUBSTITUTION DRILLS

1. How is the weather today | in California | ?
   in New York
   in Florida

2. The weather is | nice | today.
   fine
   beautiful
   perfect

3. What was the weather like yesterday? Was it | nice | ?
   sunny
   stormy
   cloudy

4. Yesterday it | rained | all day.
   snowed

5. The weather was | nice | last week.
   terrible
   awful
   miserable

6. What will the weather be like | tomorrow | ?
   the day after tomorrow
   next Sunday

7. It's going to | snow | tomorrow.
   rain
   sleet
   hail
   drizzle

8. It's | cold | today. What will the weather be like tomorrow?
   hot
   sunny
   cloudy
   windy
   foggy

9. It's been | cloudy | all morning.
foggy
chilly
warm

10. How's the weather? Is it | raining | now?
snowing
sleeting
hailing
drizzling

11. It'll probably | clear up | this afternoon.
rain
snow

12. The days are getting | hotter | .
colder
warmer
cooler
longer
shorter

13. Today is the first day of | spring | .
summer
winter
fall

14. There's a | cool breeze | this evening, isn't there?
strong wind
gusty wind

15. It's | cold | today. What's the temperature?
hot
cool
warm
freezing

16. The temperature is about | 70 degrees | .
70 degrees Fahrenheit
32° F.
zero degrees centigrade
3° C.

READING PRACTICE

Talking About the Weather

As the American author, Mark Twain, once said, "Everybody talks about the weather, but nobody does anything about it." It is true that everybody talks about the weather; it's the most common subject of conversation there is. "Isn't it a nice day?" "Do you think it will rain?" "I think it's going to snow." These are common ways of starting a conversation.

Many people think they can tell what the weather is going to be like. But they hardly ever agree with each other. One man may say, "Do you see how cloudy it is in the east? It's going to rain tomorrow." Another man will say, "Yes, it's cloudy in the east. We're going to have fine weather tomorrow."

People often look for the weather they want. When a farmer needs water, he looks for something to tell him it's going to rain; he won't believe anything else. When friends have a picnic, they are so sure the weather is going to clear up very quickly that they sit eating their lunch while it rains.

Almost everyone listens to what the weatherman says. But he doesn't always tell us what we want, and once in a while he makes a mistake. Still, he probably comes closer to being correct than anyone else.

Questions

1. What did Mark Twain say about the weather?
2. What is the most common subject of conversation?
3. Do people usually agree about the weather?
4. Do you believe that the weatherman usually gives us the correct weather news?
5. What is the weather going to be like tomorrow?

CONVERSATION

1. Talking about the weather

BOB: We're having a picnic tomorrow. Why don't you come with us?

LOUISE: I'd like to, but I think it's going to rain. The weatherman says it is.

BOB: I don't think he's right. It hasn't rained for a week and it isn't cloudy today, either.

LOUISE: But he's usually correct in his weather news.

BOB: The temperature is 80 degrees this afternoon. I'm sure we'll have fine weather for our picnic.

LOUISE: Well, I'll go, but I'll take my umbrella with me.

2. Winter weather

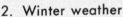

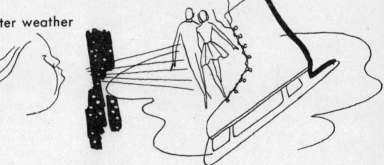

DICK: Look! It's snowing! Winter is here at last.

LARRY: It's really cold today. I'm glad I have my overcoat on.

DICK: There's ice on the lake, too. We'll be able to go skating this weekend.

LARRY: Not if it's too windy. Come on! I'm freezing.

DICK: You'll just have to learn to like it. The weather's going to be like this for the next three months.

LARRY: Then I'm going to Florida!

EXERCISES

1. Answer the following questions with short answers as shown in the example.

   Example: Is it cold today? *Yes, it is.*

   a. Did it rain yesterday? Yes, _____.

   b. Is it snowing now? No, _____.

   c. Is it cold this morning? Yes, _____.

   d. Has it cleared up yet? No, _____.

   e. Has it been cloudy all day? Yes, _____.

   f. Is it going to snow tomorrow? No, _____.

   g. Is it raining now? Yes, _____.

   h. Was it sunny yesterday? No, _____.

   i. Does it usually snow in Florida? No, _____.

   j. Is there a cool breeze today? Yes, _____.

   k. Are the days getting hotter every summer? Yes, _____.

2. Use the right word.

   Example: It's *raining.* (*rain, raining*)

   a. Yesterday it _____ all night. (*hailed, hail*)

   b. It's _____ now. (*snow, snowing*)

   c. The weather's getting _____. (*hotter, more hotter*)

   d. Is it _____? (*rain, raining*)

   e. The weather was very _____. (*nicer, nice*)

   f. It'll probably be _____ all afternoon. (*drizzle, drizzling*)

   g. There's a strong _____ this evening. (*wind, windy*)

   h. The weather will be _____ tomorrow. (*cloudy, clouds*)

   i. Has it _____ yet? (*clearing up, cleared up*)

   j. The weather was _____ last week. (*terribly, terrible*)

3. Student A adds tag questions to the following statements and Student B gives short, affirmative answers. Follow the examples.

Examples: It's been beautiful this spring.
Student A: It's been beautiful this spring, hasn't it?
Student B: Yes, it has.

There's a cool breeze today.
Student A: There's a cool breeze today, isn't there?
Student B: Yes, there is.

a. It's cold today.

b. Today is the first day of spring.

c. There's a strong wind this evening.

d. The temperature will be about 70 degrees today.

e. It'll probably clear up this afternoon.

f. It's been cloudy all morning.

g. The weather was miserable last week.

h. It snowed all day yesterday.

i. It's been cold all winter.

j. There was a terrible storm in New York.

4. Use the appropriate subject in the following sentences.

there	I
we	you
it	she
they	he

a. _____ will probably rain soon.

b. _____ don't like this freezing weather, do you?

c. _____ is a gusty wind this evening, isn't there?

d. Mary is happy. _____ has been in California where it is warm.

e. My friends and I don't like snow. _____ like warm weather.

f. Peter doesn't like the rain. _____ hopes it will clear up soon.

g. The days are long and _____ are getting longer.

h. _____ am happy to hear that the days are getting warmer.

WORD LIST

awful	freezing	sunny
breeze	gusty	temperature
centigrade	like	terrible
chilly	miserable	warm
cloudy	nice	wind
cool	perfect	windy
degree	spring	winter
Fahrenheit	stormy	zero
fall	strong	
foggy	summer	

Verb Forms

clear up, cleared up (*p. and
  p. part.*)
drizzle, drizzled (*p. and p. part.*)
hail, hailed (*p. and p. part.*)
rain, rained (*p. and p. part.*)
sleet, sleeted (*p. and p. part.*)
snow, snowed (*p. and p. part.*)

Measures

$32° =$ thirty-two degrees
$32°$ F. $=$ thirty-two degrees
  Fahrenheit
$0°$ C. $=$ zero degrees centigrade

Supplementary Word List

(Conversation and Reading Practice)

agree	nobody
author	picnic
common	skating
conversation	true
ice	umbrella
lake	weatherman

UNIT 8 TALKING ABOUT SICKNESS AND HEALTH

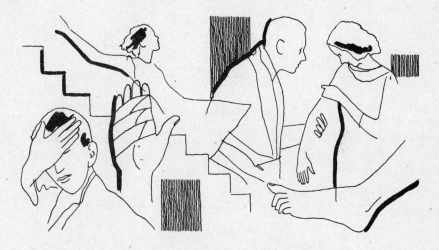

406 How are you feeling today?

407 I don't feel very well this morning.

408 I was sick yesterday, but I'm better today.

409 My fever is gone, but I still have a cough.

410 My brother has a bad headache.

411 Which of your arms is sore?

412 My right arm hurts. It hurts right here.

413 What's the matter with you?

414 I've got a pain in my back.

415 Which foot hurts? Is it the left one?

416 How did you break your leg?

417 I slipped on the stairs and fell down. I broke my leg.

418 Your right hand is swollen. Does it hurt?

419 It's bleeding. You'd better go see a doctor about that cut.

420 I hope you'll be well soon.

INTONATION

406   How are you feeling today?

407   I don't feel very well this morning.

408   I was sick yesterday, but I'm better today.

409   My fever is gone, but I still have a cough.

410   My brother has a bad headache.

411   Which of your arms is sore?

412   My right arm hurts. It hurts right here.

413   What's the matter with you?

414   I've got a pain in my back.

415   Which foot hurts? Is it the left one?

416   How did you break your leg?

417   I slipped on the stairs and fell down. I broke my leg.

418   Your right hand is swollen. Does it hurt?

419   It's bleeding. You'd better go see a doctor about that cut.

420   I hope you'll be well soon.

VERB STUDY

1. hurt
- *a.* My right arm hurts.
- *b.* Does your back hurt?
- *c.* Yesterday my right arm was hurting.
- *d.* My head hurt last night.
- *e.* I hurt my hand.
- *f.* How did you hurt your hand?
- *g.* She hurt her leg yesterday.

2. break
- *a.* How did you break your leg?
- *b.* I broke my leg yesterday afternoon.
- *c.* He breaks his leg frequently.
- *d.* I have never broken my leg.
- *e.* Has she ever broken her arm?

3. slip
- *a.* I slipped on the stairs.
- *b.* Did you slip on the stairs this morning?
- *c.* I won't slip on the stairs.

4. fall down
- *a.* I slipped on the stairs and fell down.
- *b.* Did you fall down?
- *c.* He often slips on the stairs and falls down.
- *d.* I have slipped on the stairs and fallen down many times.

5. hope, hope to
- *a.* I hope you'll be well soon.
- *b.* He hopes you'll be well soon.
- *c.* I hope to go with you tomorrow.
- *d.* He hoped to go with us today.

6. be bleeding
- *a.* Your hand is bleeding.
- *b.* My hand was bleeding last night.
- *c.* His hand isn't bleeding.

SUBSTITUTION DRILLS

1. How | are | you / they / Mr. and Mrs. Cooper | feeling today?
   ... | is | John / Mary |

1. How are
   | you
   | they
   | Mr. and Mrs. Cooper
   feeling today?

   is
   | John
   | Mary

2. I / They | don't | feel very well this morning.
   He / She | doesn't |

3. I was | sick / ill | yesterday, but I'm better today.

4. My fever is gone, but I still have | a cough / a sore throat / pains in my chest / a bad cold | .

5. My brother has a bad | headache / toothache / backache | .

6. Which of your | arms / hands / legs / feet | is sore?

7. My right | arm / leg / hand / foot / ear / eye | hurts. It hurts right here.

8. What's the matter with | you / him / her / them | ?

9. I've got a | pain / slight pain / terrible pain | in my back.

10. How did you break your | leg / arm / wrist / ankle | ?

11. I slipped on the stairs and fell down. I broke my | leg / arm / ankle / wrist | .

12. Your | right hand / thumb / finger / toe | is swollen. Does it hurt?

13. I've got a pain in my | back / neck / stomach / knee | .

14. It's bleeding. | You'd better / You better / You ought to / You should | go see a doctor about that.

15. I don't feel very well. My arm | hurts / aches | .

16. My brother is | very well / very sick / not well / healthy | .

17. I'm not feeling very well today. My | head / back / left shoulder / arm / leg | aches.

READING PRACTICE

Talking About Sickness and Health

Bobby Adams was very quiet as Dr. Smith examined him. The doctor looked at the boy's throat, took his temperature and listened to his heart. Finally, he asked Bobby's mother a few questions.

"When did Bobby begin to feel ill?"

"This morning when he got up. He said he felt too sick to go to school today."

"What did he eat for breakfast?"

"He had orange juice, two pieces of buttered toast, dry cereal, and milk."

"I see." The doctor asked Bobby, "How do you feel now, my boy?"

Bobby answered, "Terrible. I think I'm going to die."

The doctor said, "You won't die. In fact, you'll be fine by dinner time."

"Oh, Doctor! Do you really think so?" Bobby's mother looked very glad.

Dr. Smith answered, "Mrs. Adams, your son has a sickness that is very common to boys at a time like this. It comes and goes very quickly."

Mrs. Adams said, "But I don't understand."

"Today," the doctor told her, "the most important baseball game of the year is on television. If Bobby feels well enough to watch television this afternoon, and I think he does, he will be fine when the game is finished. It's the only cure I know for this sickness. Now, if you'll excuse me, I must go across the street to see the Morton's boy, Alfred. He seems to have the same thing Bobby has today."

Questions

1. How did Dr. Smith examine Bobby?
2. What had Bobby eaten for breakfast?
3. Did the doctor think Bobby would get well?
4. How did Bobby say he felt?
5. Have you ever had a sickness like Bobby Adams'?

CONVERSATION

1. Appointment with the doctor

NURSE: The doctor will see you in a minute, Mr. Lewis. While you're waiting, you can answer some questions.

MR. LEWIS: But, nurse, you don't understand. I only want to see the doctor about . . .

NURSE: I know you want to see the doctor, Mr. Lewis. And you will in just a few minutes. But first I must ask you about your health.

MR. LEWIS: I'm very healthy.

NURSE: You are? Then why are you here?

MR. LEWIS: I want to pay the doctor for my wife's operation last month.

NURSE: You do? Why didn't you say so? Go right in!

2. A broken left arm

MOTHER: Billy! What's the matter? Are you hurt?

BILLY: I slipped on the stairs and fell down. I think my arm is broken.

MOTHER: Oh! I hope not. Which arm is it?

BILLY: The left one. It hurts right here.

MOTHER: Let me see. I don't think it's broken but we're going to see the doctor right now.

BILLY: I'm glad it wasn't my right arm. That's the one I need for baseball.

EXERCISES

1. Complete the following sentences.

   Example: How are you *feeling* today? (*feeling, feel, do*)

   a. I _____ feel well today. (*doesn't, don't, am not*)

   b. My headache _____ gone. (*are, do, is*)

   c. My sister _____ a fever. (*have, has, makes*)

   d. My arm _____. (*hurt, hurts, do hurt*)

   e. Did you _____ your arm? (*broke, breaks, break*)

   f. I _____ and fell down. (*slip, slips, slipped*)

   g. She often _____ and falls. (*slip, slips, slipped*)

   h. Mary _____ you'll feel better soon. (*hope, hopes, hopes to*)

   i. My leg _____ bleeding. (*are, is, aren't*)

   j. Have you ever _____ your leg? (*break, broke, broken*)

   k. I _____ go with her. (*hope to, hopes to, hopes*)

   l. I've _____ a pain in my back. (*get, got, getting*)

   m. You'd _____ go see a doctor. (*good, better, well*)

   n. Your thumb is _____. (*swells, swell, swollen*)

2. Complete the sentences with the appropriate word from the list.

coughing	better	sick	matter
had to	sore throat	ached	pains

   a. I felt very _____ yesterday.

   b. I was _____ a great deal and I had a _____.

   c. I _____ call a doctor.

   d. He asked me what was the _____.

   e. I told him my throat and my head _____.

   f. I'm feeling a little _____ today.

   g. My fever is gone and so are the _____ in my throat.

3. Complete these sentences with the appropriate word from the list below.

fell   pain   break   hurts
swollen   bleeding   ought to

    a. My friend slipped and _____ down the stairs.

    b. His leg was _____ and _____.

    c. I told him he _____ see a doctor.

    d. He said to the doctor, "My leg _____ very much."

    e. "I hope I didn't _____ it."

    f. He feels better today, but he still has a _____ in his leg.

4. Use contractions in the following sentences.

    Example: I have got a headache. *I've got a headache.*

        a. I have got a terrible toothache.
        b. He has got a broken leg.
        c. You had better see a doctor about that.
        d. She does not feel well this morning.
        e. He should not go to work with a bad cold.
        f. I do not feel better today.
        g. My fever is gone.
        h. My arm is broken.

5. Change the following to negative sentences.

    Example: I feel well. I *don't* feel well.

        a. John has a fever.
        b. I've got a headache.
        c. I hurt my leg when I fell down.
        d. Have you ever had a sore throat?
        e. Did you have a toothache yesterday?
        f. Are you feeling sick today?
        g. Should you see a doctor about that?
        h. Did she feel better this morning?

WORD LIST

ankle	finger	sick
arm	foot, feet	slight
back	hand	soon
backache	head	sore
bad	headache	stomach
chest	healthy	swollen
cold	ill	throat
cough	knee	thumb
cut	leg	toe
ear	neck	toothache
eye	pain	which of
fever	shoulder	wrist

Verb Forms

ache, ached (*p. and p. part.*)
bleed, bled (*p. and p. part.*)
break, broke (*p.*), broken
   (*p. part.*)
fall down, fell down (*p.*),
   fallen down (*p. part.*)
hurt, hurt (*p. and p. part.*)
slip, slipped (*p. and p. part.*)

Expressions

be better
feel well
had better
have got, has got

Supplementary Word List

(Conversation and Reading Practice)

baseball	game
common	heart
cure	important
enough	operation
examined	pay

UNIT 9 TALKING ABOUT DAILY HABITS

421   I get out of bed about 7 o'clock every morning.

422   After getting up, I go into the bathroom and take a shower.

423   Then, I shave, brush my teeth and comb my hair.

424   After brushing my teeth, I put on my clothes.

425   After that, I go downstairs to the kitchen to have breakfast.

426   After eating breakfast, I go back upstairs again.

427   Then, it's usually time to wake up my little brother.

428   He can't dress himself yet because he's too young.

429   I wash his face and hands, and then I dress him.

430   He tries to button his own shirt, but he can't do it.

431   My little brother takes a bath before he goes to bed at night.

432   He always forgets to wash behind his ears.

433   I'm always tired when I come home from work.

434   At bedtime, I take off my clothes and put on my pajamas.

435   I get into bed at about 11:30, and go right off to sleep.

INTONATION

421   I get out of bed about 7 o'clock every morning.

422   After getting up, I go into the bathroom and take a shower.

423   Then, I shave, brush my teeth and comb my hair.

424   After brushing my teeth, I put on my clothes.

425   After that, I go downstairs to the kitchen to have breakfast.

426   After eating breakfast, I go back upstairs again.

427   Then, it's usually time to wake up my little brother.

428   He can't dress himself yet because he's too young.

429   I wash his face and hands, and then I dress him.

430   He tries to button his own shirt, but he can't do it.

431   My little brother takes a bath before he goes to bed at night.

432   He always forgets to wash behind his ears.

433   I'm always tired when I come home from work.

434   At bedtime, I take off my clothes and put on my pajamas.

435   I get into bed at about eleven thirty, and go right off to sleep.

VERB STUDY

1. **get out of bed, get into bed**
   a. I get out of bed at about 7 o'clock every morning.
   b. My brother gets out of bed at 11 o'clock in the morning.
   c. I got out of bed at 7 o'clock yesterday morning.
   d. I get into bed at about 11:30 every night.
   e. John gets into bed at midnight every night.

2. **put on, take off**
   a. After brushing his teeth, he puts on his clothes.
   b. Yesterday I put on my clothes at about 7 o'clock.
   c. At bedtime, I take off my clothes and put on my pajamas.
   d. After he takes a bath, he puts on his pajamas.

3. **shave**
   a. I shave every morning.
   b. I've already shaved twice today.
   c. I shaved after breakfast yesterday morning.
   d. He shaves every Monday morning.
   e. He's shaving right now.

4. **brush (one's) teeth**
   a. I brush my teeth every morning.
   b. Last night I brushed my teeth after dinner.
   c. He brushes his teeth after breakfast, lunch, and dinner.
   d. I've brushed my teeth three times today.
   e. She's brushing her teeth right now, isn't she?

5. **comb (one's) hair**
   a. After I brush my teeth, I comb my hair.
   b. I combed my hair three times yesterday.
   c. She combs her hair many times each day.
   d. I've combed my hair this way for a long time.
   e. He's combing his hair right now.

6. **dress (one's self)**
   a. He can't dress himself yet, because he's too young.
   b. Their little daughter dresses herself already.
   c. He dressed himself, and then he combed his hair.

7. **button**
   a. He tries to button his shirt, but he can't do it.
   b. He buttoned his shirt, and then he combed his hair.

SUBSTITUTION DRILLS

1. I | get out of bed / jump out of bed / get up | at about 7 o'clock every morning.

2. After getting up, | I go / he goes / John goes | into the bathroom.

3. John goes into the bathroom and | takes a shower / takes a hot shower / takes a cold shower / takes a bath / bathes | .

4. After | getting up / taking a shower / combing my hair / getting dressed / bathing | , I shave and brush my teeth.

5. After taking a shower, John shaves and | brushes his teeth / combs his hair / puts on his clothes | .

6. After | taking a shower / brushing his teeth / combing his hair / washing his face and hands | , John puts on his clothes.

7. After that, | I / we / they | go / she / John | goes | downstairs to the kitchen to have breakfast.

8. John goes downstairs to the | kitchen | .
   | dining room |
   | living room |

9. After eating breakfast, | I go back | upstairs again.
   | she goes back |
   | John goes back |

10. Then it's usually time to | wake up my little brother | .
    | dress my little brother |
    | get my little brother up |
    | give my little brother a bath |
    | wash my little brother's face and hands |

11. Then it's usually time to wake up | my | little brother.
    | his |
    | her |
    | their |
    | John's |

12. He tries to button his own | shirt | , but he can't do it.
    | pants |
    | coat |
    | sweater |
    | jacket |
    | raincoat |

13. I'm always | tired | when I come home from work.
    | sleepy |
    | happy |
    | sad |
    | hungry |

14. He can't | dress himself | yet because he's too young.
    | bathe himself |
    | brush his own teeth |
    | comb his own hair |
    | fix his own breakfast |

15.

He	can't dress	himself	yet because	he's	too young.
She		herself		she's	
They		themselves		they're	
You		yourself		you're	
I		myself		I'm	
We		ourselves		we're	

16. At bedtime,

I take off my	clothes and	put on my	pajamas.
he takes off his		puts on his	
she takes off her		puts on her	
they take off their		put on their	
you take off your		put on your	

17.

I get	into bed at about 11:30, and	go	right off to sleep.
He gets		goes	
She gets		goes	
They get		go	
You get		go	
We get		go	

18. I'm always tired

when I come home
after work
at bedtime

.

19.

After breakfast
After that
Then

, I wake up my brother.

20. I'm

always
usually
sometimes
almost always
hardly ever
never

hungry when I get up in the morning.

READING PRACTICE

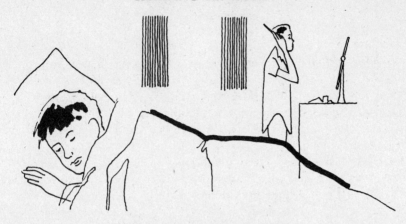

Talking About Daily Habits

I think the most terrible thing in life for my little brother is getting up in the morning. He is almost sick when my mother calls, "Herbert! It's seven o'clock! Get up!"

Herby answers, "I'm coming!" and goes right back to sleep.

I'm not at all like my brother. I don't like to go to bed at night but I don't mind getting up in the morning. I usually wake up before my mother calls me. I jump out of bed and go into the bathroom to take my shower. I get dressed, brush my teeth, comb my hair, and get ready to go downstairs for breakfast as soon as my mother calls.

But not Herby. He just sleeps. A military band in our bedroom could not wake him up. I call him and say, "Get up! Mom will be up here to pull you out of bed if you don't get up immediately!"

But he just sleeps. After calling a few more times my mother has to come upstairs and pull Herby out of bed. He always says, "I was going to get up in another minute. Really I was."

It's that way every day with my little brother. Perhaps some day he'll learn to get up on time, but I really don't think so.

Questions

1. What doesn't Herby like to do?
2. What doesn't his brother like to do?
3. What does Herby's brother do before his mother calls in the morning?
4. What does Herby say when his mother pulls him out of bed?
5. Are you like Herby or his brother?

CONVERSATION

Bedtime

MOTHER: Children! It's your bedtime. Go upstairs and go to bed.

MARY: Oh, Mother! Do we have to? It's still early.

BEN: Yes, and it's Friday night. There's no school tomorrow.

MOTHER: Yes, but tomorrow we have to get up early and go shopping.

MARY: I forgot that. Okay, I'll go to bed without arguing. I like to shop.

BEN: Do I have to take a bath tonight, Mom?

MOTHER: Of course you do. And don't forget to wash behind your ears.

MARY: Do I have clean pajamas, Mother?

MOTHER: Yes. They're in your closet. Be sure to brush your teeth, Mary.

MARY: I will. And I'll comb my hair, too.

BEN: Good night, everybody. See you tomorrow.

MOTHER: Good night. Don't forget to open your bedroom window before you go to sleep.

MARY: We won't. Good night, Mom.

EXERCISES

1. Student A asks the following questions, and Student B gives complete answers, using the information in parentheses.

   Examples: Student A: When do you go to school? (*at 9:00*)
   Student B: *I go to school at 9:00.*

   Student A: When do you go to work? (*after I eat breakfast*)
   Student B: *I go to work after I eat breakfast.*

   a. What time do you get out of bed every morning? (*at about 7 o'clock*)

   b. When do you brush your teeth? (*after taking a shower*)

   c. When do you go downstairs? (*after I put on my clothes*)

   d. Where do you eat breakfast? (*downstairs in the kitchen*)

   e. Why can't your brother dress himself yet? (*because he's too young*)

   f. How do you feel when you come home from work? (*tired and hungry*)

   g. When do you put on your pajamas? (*at bedtime*)

   h. What time do you get into bed? (*about 11:30*)

2. Complete the following sentences with the appropriate words from the list.

put on	go off	wake up	get out
go into	getting up	get into	take off

   a. I _____ of bed at 7 a.m.

   b. After _____, I take a shower.

   c. After that, I _____ my clothes.

   d. Before I leave the house, I _____ my brother.

   e. When he is dressed, we _____ the kitchen for breakfast.

   f. At bedtime, I _____ my clothes and put on my pajamas.

   g. After that, I go upstairs and _____ bed.

   h. I usually _____ right _____ to sleep.

3. Insert the word in parentheses in the proper position in the sentence. Follow the examples.

> *Examples:* My brother can't button his jacket. (*still*)
> *My brother still can't button his jacket.*
>
> My brother can't fix his own breakfast. (*yet*)
> *My brother can't fix his own breakfast yet.*
>
> I shave every day. (*always*)
> *I always shave every day.*
>
> I eat breakfast at 7 o'clock. (*usually*)
> *I usually eat breakfast at 7 o'clock.*

a. My little brother can't dress himself. (*still*)

b. My little brother can't bathe himself. (*yet*)

c. I get up at 7:00 every morning. (*always*)

d. He brushes his teeth after he shaves. (*usually*)

e. He hasn't combed his hair. (*still*)

f. He hasn't washed his face and hands. (*yet*)

g. I'm hungry when I wake up. (*always*)

h. I'm tired when I come home from work. (*usually*)

4. Complete the sentences with the proper form of the pronoun from the list.

himself	yourself	her	I	they
herself	my	their	he	you
themselves	his	your	she	we

a. I take off _____ clothes before I go to bed.

b. My little brother tried to button _____ own shirt.

c. He can't dress _____ yet.

d. She usually combs _____ own hair.

e. She still cannot bathe _____.

f. The children tried to put their jackets on _____.

g. You can dress _____, can't you?

h. In the morning the children took off _____ own pajamas.

i. Do you eat _____ breakfast in the dining room?

j. After the boys get up, _____ shave and brush their teeth.

k. John goes downstairs where _____ fixes breakfast.

l. After John and I get dressed, _____ eat breakfast together in the kitchen.

m. Then _____ go back upstairs to wake up my sister.

n. I help her get dressed because _____ is still too young to dress herself.

o. You help your little brother, don't _____?

5. **Use the right verb to complete the sentences.**

Example: I *get* dressed. (*get, give*)

a. I _____ my teeth. (*brush, button*)

b. I _____ my hair. (*comb, shave*)

c. I _____ breakfast. (*fix, put*)

d. I _____ my shirt. (*give, button*)

e. I _____ my face. (*comb, shave*)

f. I _____ my clothes. (*wash, bathe*)

g. I _____ a shower. (*wash, take*)

h. I _____ into bed. (*jump, take*)

i. I _____ on my pajamas. (*put, take*)

j. I _____ off my jacket. (*put, take*)

WORD LIST

again	herself	pants
bathroom	himself	raincoat
because	hungry	sad
bed	jacket	sweater
bedtime	living room	teeth
behind	myself	themselves
clothes	off	tired
downstairs	ourselves	upstairs
face	own	yourself
hair	pajamas	

Verb Forms

bathe, bathed (*p. and p. part.*)
brush, brushed (*p. and p. part.*)
button, buttoned (*p. and p. part.*)
comb, combed (*p. and p. part.*)
fix, fixed (*p. and p. part.*)
go back, went back (*p.*),
   gone back (*p. part.*)
jump, jumped (*p. and p. part.*)
put on, put on (*p. and p. part.*)
shave, shaved (*p. and p. part.*)
take off, took off (*p.*),
   taken off (*p. part.*)
try, tried (*p. and p. part.*)
wash, washed (*p. and p. part.*)

Expressions

fix breakfast
get into bed
get out of bed
give a bath
jump out of bed
take a bath
take a shower

Supplementary Word List

(Conversation and Reading Practice)

bedroom
military band
pull
shop

10 GETTING OTHER PEOPLE'S OPINIONS AND IDEAS

436 What do you think? Is that right?

437 Certainly. You're absolutely right about that.

438 I think you're mistaken about that.

439 I like hot weather best.

440 Personally, I prefer winter weather.

441 Do you think it's going to rain tomorrow?

442 I don't know whether it will rain or not.

443 In my opinion, that's an excellent idea.

444 Why is Mr. Cooper so tired? Do you have any idea?

445 He's tired because he worked hard all day today.

446 What do you think of my children?

447 I think you have very attractive children.

448 Please give me your frank opinion.

449 Do you really want to know what I think?

450 Of course I want to know what your opinion is!

INTONATION

436   What do you think? Is that right?

437   Certainly. You're absolutely right about that.

438   I think you're mistaken about that.

439   I like hot weather best.

440   Personally, I prefer winter weather.

441   Do you think it's going to rain tomorrow?

442   I don't know whether it will rain or not.

443   In my opinion, that's an excellent idea.

444   Why is Mr. Cooper so tired? Do you have any idea?

445   He's tired because he worked hard all day today.

446   What do you think of my children?

447   I think you have very attractive children.

448   Please give me your frank opinion.

449   Do you really want to know what I think?

450   Of course I want to know what your opinion is!

VERB STUDY

1. **think**
   a. What do you think?
   b. He thinks you're absolutely right about that.
   c. He thought you were right about that.
   d. We think you're mistaken about that.
   e. Do you really want to know what I think?

2. **think of**
   a. What do you think of my children?
   b. I think a lot of Mr. Cooper.
   c. You thought a lot of Mr. Cooper, didn't you?
   d. What does she think of my French accent?

3. **prefer**
   a. Personally, I prefer winter weather.
   b. She prefers summer weather.
   c. He likes winter weather best, but she prefers summer weather.
   d. Which do you prefer?
   e. Which does he prefer?

4. **work**
   a. He worked hard all day.
   b. He always works hard every day.
   c. I work hard , too.
   d. My friends work eight hours every day.
   e. I've worked in New York for ten years.
   f. Yesterday she worked at home all day.
   g. Last year he was working in California.
   h. Has she always worked in New York?

5. **be mistaken**
   a. I think you're mistaken about that.
   b. We thought you were mistaken about that.
   c. Isn't he mistaken about that?
   d. I'm mistaken about that.

SUBSTITUTION DRILLS

1. What do you think? Is that | right / wrong / correct / incorrect | ?

2. | Certainly / Of course / Naturally | . You're absolutely right about that.

3. | I think / She thinks / John thinks | you're mistaken about that.

4. | You're / You're not / You aren't / He's / He's not / He isn't | mistaken about that.

5. | Aren't you / Isn't she / Isn't John | mistaken about that?

6. I like | hot weather / winter weather / summertime / sunshine | best.

7. Personally, I | prefer / love / like / enjoy | winter weather.

8. Do you | think / suppose / feel / believe | it's going to rain tomorrow?

9. I don't know whether | it will rain | or not.
    John will leave today
    I will see him
    I'll enjoy the movie

10. In my opinion, that's | an excellent | idea.
    a wonderful
    a marvelous
    a good

11. Why is Mr. Cooper so | tired | ? Do you have any idea?
    happy
    sad
    excited
    angry
    healthy

12. I don't know why. Maybe it's because he | worked hard all day | .
    finished working
      early today
    finished working
      late today
    got a letter from his
      friend
    didn't have lunch
      today
    always eats good
      food

13. What do you think of my | children | ?
    pet dog
    garden
    story
    poem

14.
| I think |
| Personally, I think |
| In my opinion |
| Personally, I'm of the opinion that |

you have very attractive children.

15. Please give me your
| frank |
| honest |
| medical |
opinion.

16. Do you really want to know what
| I think |
| she thinks |
| John thinks |
?

17. Of course I want to know what your
| opinion |
| judgment |
| conclusion |
| recommendation |
is.

18. I like geography, but I prefer
| history |
| art |
| literature |
| music |
| medicine |
| mathematics |
| religion |
.

19. Mr. Cooper is happy because today is
| his birthday |
| his wedding anniversary |
| the first day of spring |
| a holiday |
.

READING PRACTICE

Getting Other People's Opinions and Ideas

When I was a child there were some people whose ideas I respected. My Uncle John, I thought, knew everything about the world; he had traveled and seen all there was to see. I believed anything he told me about places like Japan, Australia, and Brazil. When I wanted to know anything about baseball I asked our neighbor, Mr. Fulton; there wasn't anything he didn't know about that game. My teacher, Miss Ellis, was an expert on nature and I always believed all of the things she told our class about plants and animals.

When I was sixteen years old I got the idea that my parents, while they were very nice people and I loved them, really didn't know very much. I, of course, knew everything. Then, when I was eighteen, I realized my mother and father had learned a lot in just two years. I now respected their opinions on different subjects. It took two years of growing up for me to realize that they had had these opinions and ideas all the time.

Some people have an opinion on every subject. Others have none. The best kind is the person who studies the subject before giving an answer to the question, "What do you think?"

Questions

1. What do you think of a person who has an opinion on every subject?
2. Do you think Uncle John knew everything about the world?
3. Do you suppose that Miss Ellis was really an expert on nature?
4. Why did the boy think his parents had learned a lot in two years?
5. Do you like to give your opinion on different subjects?

CONVERSATION

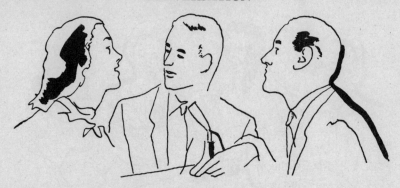

INTERVIEWER: Mr. Smith, we are very happy to have you on our television program this evening.

MR. SMITH: I am glad to be here.

INTERVIEWER: Miss Fisher and I both have questions for you. We'd like to know your opinion. Miss Fisher, do you want to ask the first question?

MISS FISHER: Thank you. Mr. Smith, what do you think of our morning newspaper? Would you say it gives us all the latest news?

MR. SMITH: Yes, I would say so. I think it is a very good newspaper.

INTERVIEWER: What is your opinion of television? Do you think that all the programs are good?

MR. SMITH: No, I don't. Some of the programs are interesting, but others could be better.

MISS FISHER: Please give me your frank opinion about our schools, Mr. Smith. Do you believe our teachers are doing a good job?

MR. SMITH: Yes, I do. I believe our schools are excellent.

INTERVIEWER: What about music? What do you think of modern music?

MR. SMITH: I guess some of it is good. I don't always understand it. Personally, I prefer the symphonies of Beethoven.

INTERVIEWER: We'd like to talk more, Mr. Smith, but we have no time. Miss Fisher and I want to thank you for being with us on our program this evening.

MISS FISHER: I am sure our television audience has enjoyed listening to your opinions. Thank you, and good night.

MR. SMITH: It was my pleasure.

EXERCISES

1. Begin each of the following questions with the phrase in parentheses. Follow the example. Use contractions wherever possible.

   Example: Will you go to school tonight? (*do you think*)
   Do you think you'll go to school tonight?

   a. Is it going to rain tomorrow? (*do you think*)
   b. Are you mistaken about that? (*don't you think*)
   c. Was Mr. Cooper tired because he worked hard all day? (*do you suppose*)
   d. Will I enjoy the movie? (*do you believe*)
   e. Can you give me your honest opinion? (*do you feel*)
   f. Is Mr. Cooper angry because he didn't have lunch today? (*don't you feel*)
   g. Is Mr. Cooper happy because today is his birthday? (*don't you believe*)
   h. Does Mr. Cooper prefer warm weather? (*don't you suppose*)
   i. Does she love winter weather? (*do you think*)
   j. Did he work hard all day? (*do you believe*)

2. Answer the following questions using the expression "I don't know whether . . . or not" as shown in the examples. Use contractions wherever possible.

   Examples: Are you going to school tonight?
   I don't know whether I'm going to school tonight or not.

   Does John enjoy school?
   I don't know whether John enjoys school or not.

   a. Will it rain tomorrow?
   b. Will John enjoy the movie?
   c. Will John give you his honest opinion?
   d. Will you see Mr. Cooper next Sunday?
   e. Is she mistaken about that?
   f. Does Mr. Cooper prefer warm weather?
   g. Will you finish working early today?
   h. Did she have lunch yet?
   i. Does John always eat good food?

3. Complete the following sentences with the correct word from the list below.

like	judgment	correct
wonderful	wrong	naturally

   a. Give me your opinion. I really want to know your _____.

   b. We prefer sunshine. We _____ hot weather best.

   c. I think finishing work early before a holiday is an excellent idea. In my opinion, that will be _____.

   d. I think John is mistaken about that. Do you also believe he is _____?

   e. Your conclusion is absolutely right about that. I know you are _____.

   f. Of course I will give you my frank opinion. _____, I will be honest with you.

4. Answer the following questions with "yes" and "no."

Example: Do you understand the lesson? *Yes, I do. No, I don't.*

   a. Is Mr. Cooper tired?
   b. Do you like my pet dog?
   c. Do you want to know what I think?
   d. Does she like music?
   e. Am I sad?
   f. Are we happy?
   g. Was he working yesterday?
   h. Were we at home?
   i. Did you enjoy the winter?
   j. Did you think a lot of Mr. Cooper?
   k. Does he like my accent?
   l. Is Mary always so happy?
   m. Am I mistaken?
   n. Is Mr. Cooper working late tonight?

WORD LIST

angry	honest	pet
art	idea	poem
attractive	incorrect	recommendation
certainly	judgment	religion
conclusion	literature	so
excellent	marvelous	story
excited	mathematics	summertime
food	medical	sunshine
frank	medicine	whether
garden	music	why
good, better, best	naturally	wonderful
holiday	personally	wrong

Verb Forms

enjoy, enjoyed (*p. and p. part.*)
love, loved (*p. and p. part.*)
prefer, preferred (*p. and p. part.*)
suppose, supposed (*p. and p. part.*)

Expressions

be mistaken
get a letter
give an opinion
of course

Supplementary Word List

(Conversation and Reading Practice)

animals	nature
baseball	plants
expert	realized
game	respected
interviewer	symphonies
job	traveled
modern	

REVIEW TWO

1. Verbs: Future action with BE GOING TO and WILL

Change these sentences to future form with "tomorrow."

a. This morning I got up at 7 o'clock. (*tomorrow*)

b. Yesterday I had breakfast at 9 o'clock.

c. Last night I went to the movies with a friend of mine.

d. We had dinner at home last night.

e. This morning I got dressed quickly.

f. I had toast and coffee for breakfast this morning.

g. My brother got up later than I did this morning.

h. Yesterday I finished working at 5:30 in the afternoon.

i. My sister went to sleep immediately last night.

j. My parents left the house at 10 o'clock yesterday morning.

k. It rained all day yesterday.

l. There was a cool breeze last night.

m. Last week it snowed.

n. I don't feel well today.

o. My little brother took a bath before he went to bed last night.

p. Last night we were tired when we came home from work.

q. Did it rain yesterday?

r. Was he sick yesterday?

s. The weather was very nice yesterday.

t. She went out for lunch at 12 noon yesterday.

u. Did you have dinner at home last night?

v. When I got sleepy last night, I went to bed.

w. After breakfast this morning I got ready to go to work.

x. Mrs. Cooper went to sleep at about 11:30 last night.

y. My brother wakes up at 7 o'clock.

z. She got dressed at 6:30 yesterday morning.

2. Verbs: Negative future action

Change these sentences to future form (negative) with "tomorrow."

a. I didn't get up at 6 o'clock this morning. (*tomorrow*)

b. My birthday was yesterday.

c. We didn't have dinner at home last night.

d. I eat dinner every day at 8 p.m.

e. I watch television for an hour every evening.

f. Last year we used to work from 9 a.m. until 5:30 p.m.

g. This morning I measured the windows to see how wide they are.

h. I was able to go to sleep immediately last night.

i. They bought the house on the corner.

j. My cousin got married yesterday.

3. Practice with questions

Write the proper question for each answer.

a. _____? Yes, I got up at 6 o'clock.

b. _____? No, I'm still single.

c. _____? They've been married for quite a few years.

d. _____? No, they don't know when the wedding will be.

e. _____? The weather is nice today.

f. _____? No, it's not raining now.

g. _____? It's about 70° this afternoon.

4. Conversation Practice

a. Talking about the weather.

You and your friend, Fred, are talking about the weather. You ask Fred how the weather is, and he tells you. Then, you ask about how the weather was yesterday, and what the weather will be tomorrow.

You:

Fred:

_ _ _ _ _ _ _ _ _ _ _ _

b. Talking about sickness and health.

You meet Mr. Cooper. Mr. Cooper doesn't feel well. Mr. Cooper's brother doesn't feel well, either. His brother has a pain in his back. Mr. Cooper sees your hand. Your hand is swollen. Mr. Cooper recommends you see a doctor.

You:

Mr. Cooper:

— — — — — — — — — — — —

5. Answer the questions

a. What time are you going to get up tomorrow morning?

b. What are you going to have for breakfast tomorrow morning?

c. What do you do when you get sleepy at night?

d. What time will you be able to go to sleep tomorrow night?

e. How many brothers and sisters do you have?

f. Where do your brothers and sisters live?

g. Do you like hot weather or cold weather?

h. Do you think it will rain tomorrow?

i. Do you comb your hair several times a day?

j. How many days a week do you work?

k. Do you know why Mr. Cooper is so tired?

6. Sentence Review

Study and review Base Sentences 376 to 450.

WORD INDEX

TO BOOK 3

The following is a listing of words introduced in Book Three. Each word in the listing is accompanied by the sentence in which the word was introduced in the text. The number shown in parentheses indicates the unit in which the sentence appeared.

A

able to	If you are able to, will you call me tomorrow?	(2)
aches	I don't feel very well. My arm aches.	(8)
across	The restaurant is across the street from the hotel.	(3)
advise	Would you please advise him that I'm here?	(2)
again	After eating breakfast, I go back upstairs again.	(9)
ahead	It's two blocks straight ahead.	(3)
airport	Can you tell me where the airport is?	(3)
angry	Why is Mr. Cooper so angry?	(10)
ankle	How did you break your ankle?	(8)
anniversary	When is your grandparents' wedding anniversary?	(4)
apartment	What size apartment do you own?	(1)
approximately	Approximately how long have they been married?	(4)
argue	Please don't argue with me now. I'm very busy.	(2)
arms	Which of your arms is sore?	(8)
around	The school is just around the corner.	(3)
art	I like geography, but I prefer art.	(10)
as . . . as	This window is just as wide as that one.	(1)
attractive	I think you have very attractive children.	(10)
awful	The weather was awful last week.	(7)
awfully	It's not awfully heavy, but I don't know the exact weight.	(1)

B

baby	They had a baby last month.	(4)
bachelor	My cousin is a bachelor.	(4)
back	I've got a pain in my back.	(8)
backache	My brother has a bad backache.	(8)
bad	My brother has a bad headache.	(8)
bank	Which direction is it to the bank?	(3)
basement	The restaurant is in the basement.	(3)
bath	My little brother takes a bath before he goes to bed at night.	(9)
bathes	John goes into the bathroom and bathes.	(9)
bathroom	After getting up, I go into the bathroom and take a shower.	(9)
beautiful	What beautiful trees those are!	(5)
because	He can't dress himself yet because he's too young.	(9)

bedtime	At bedtime, I take off my clothes and put on my pajamas.	(9)
beg	I beg your pardon.	(3)
behind	He always forgets to wash behind his ears.	(9)
best	I like hot weather best.	(10)
better	It's bleeding. You'd better go see a doctor about that cut.	(8)
better	I was sick yesterday, but I'm better today.	(8)
bigger	This pencil is bigger than that one.	(1)
bleeding	It's bleeding.	(8)
bother	Please don't bother me now. I'm very busy.	(2)
bought	Who bought that new house down the street from you?	(5)
box	Would you help me lift this heavy box?	(2)
break	How did you break your leg?	(8)
breeze	There's a cool breeze this evening.	(7)
bright	My book has a bright red cover.	(1)
bring	Please bring me those magazines.	(2)
broke	I slipped on the stairs and fell down. I broke my leg.	(8)
brush	Then, I shave, brush my teeth and comb my hair.	(9)
building	They're building a new building up the street from me.	(5)
building	They're building a new house up the street from me.	(5)
built	All of those houses have been built in the last ten years.	(5)
button	He tries to button his own shirt, but he can't do it.	(9)
buy	If you buy that home, will you spend the rest of your life there?	(5)

C

camera	What color is your camera?	(1)
captain	Excuse me, Captain.	(3)
carry	Would you help me carry this heavy box?	(2)
centigrade	The temperature is about zero degrees centigrade.	(7)
certainly	Certainly. You're absolutely right about that.	(10)
changes	There have been a lot of changes here in the last 20 years.	(5)
chest	My fever is gone, but I still have pains in my chest.	(8)
childhood	My friend spent his childhood in California.	(5)
chilly	It's been chilly all morning.	(7)
church	Which direction is it to the church?	(3)
clear up	It'll probably clear up this afternoon.	(7)
closet	Hang up my coat in the closet, will you please?	(2)
clothes	After brushing my teeth, I put on my clothes.	(9)
cloudy	It's been cloudy all morning.	(7)
cold	My fever is gone, but I still have a bad cold.	(8)
colonel	Excuse me, Colonel.	(3)
color	What color is your book?	(1)
comb	Then, I shave, brush my teeth and comb my hair.	(9)
conclusion	Of course I want to know what your conclusion is.	(10)
cool	There's a cool breeze this evening.	(7)
corner	Turn right at the next corner.	(3)

cough	My fever is gone, but I still have a cough.	(8)
count	Please count the chairs in that room.	(2)
couple	A young married couple moved in next door to us.	(5)
cover	My book has a dark blue cover.	(1)
crack of dawn	John will probably wake up at the crack of dawn.	(6)
cut	It's bleeding. You better go see a doctor about that cut.	(8)

D

dark	My book has a dark blue cover.	(1)
degrees	The temperature is about 70 degrees.	(7)
department store	There used to be a department store on the corner.	(5)
developments	There have been a lot of developments here in the last 20 years.	(5)
diamond	What size diamond do you own?	(1)
died	She's a widow. Her husband died last year.	(4)
direction	Which direction is it to the theater?	(3)
down	The restaurant is down those stairs.	(3)
downstairs	After that, I go downstairs to the kitchen to have breakfast.	(9)
drive	It's a long drive from here to the university.	(3)
drizzle	It's going to drizzle tomorrow.	(7)
drugstore	There used to be a drugstore on the corner.	(5)

E

each other	We all know each other pretty well.	(5)
ear	My right ear hurts.	(8)
eggs	I'll probably have eggs and toast for breakfast.	(6)
elderly	An elderly man rented the big white house.	(5)
elephant	How much does that elephant weigh?	(1)
engaged	Your niece is engaged, isn't she?	(4)
enjoy	Personally, I enjoy winter weather.	(10)
excellent	In my opinion, that's an excellent idea.	(10)
excited	Why is Mr. Cooper so excited?	(10)
eye	My right eye hurts.	(8)

F

face	I wash his face and hands, and then I dress him.	(9)
Fahrenheit	The temperature is about 70 degrees Fahrenheit.	(7)
fairly	It's fairly heavy, but I don't know the exact weight.	(1)
fall	Today is the first day of fall.	(7)
farm	I grew up on a farm.	(5)
favor	Will you do me a favor?	(2)
feel	Do you feel it's going to rain tomorrow?	(10)
feeling	How are you feeling today?	(8)
feels	This material feels soft.	(1)
feet	Which of your feet is sore?	(8)
feet	That street is only 900 feet long.	(1)
fell down	I slipped on the stairs and fell down.	(8)

fever	My fever is gone, but I still have a cough.	(8)
finger	Your finger is swollen.	(8)
fix	He can't fix his own breakfast yet because he's too young.	(9)
flowers	What beautiful flowers those are!	(5)
foggy	It's foggy today.	(7)
food	I don't know why. Maybe it's because he always eats good food.	(10)
foot	Which foot hurts?	(8)
forks	Please pick up those knives and forks, will you?	(2)
frank	Please give me your frank opinion.	(10)
freezing	It's freezing today.	(7)
friendly	Are your neighbors very friendly?	(5)

G

garden	What do you think of my garden?	(10)
get	Get me a hammer from the kitchen, will you?	(2)
go back	After eating breakfast, I go back upstairs again.	(9)
got	I've got a pain in my back.	(8)
got	I don't know why. Maybe it's because he got a letter from his friend.	(10)
grandchild	Our grandchild wants to get married in June.	(4)
grandchildren	Their grandchildren are grown up now.	(4)
granddaughter	My granddaughter got married in 1945.	(4)
grandfather	My grandfather got married in 1931.	(4)
grandmother	My grandmother got married in 1945.	(4)
grandparents'	When is your grandparents' wedding anniversary?	(4)
grandson	My grandson got married in 1945.	(4)
grew up	I grew up right here in this neighborhood.	(5)
grocery	There used to be a grocery store on the corner.	(5)
grown up	Their grandchildren are grown up now.	(4)
grow up	Where did you grow up?	(5)
gusty	There's a gusty wind this evening, isn't there?	(7)

H

hail	It's going to hail tomorrow.	(7)
hair	Then, I shave, brush my teeth and comb my hair.	(9)
hammer	Get me a hammer from the kitchen, will you?	(2)
hand	Your right hand is swollen.	(8)
hand	Please hand me those magazines.	(2)
hang up	Hang up my coat in the closet, will you please?	(2)
happen to	Do you happen to know Mr. Cooper's telephone number?	(3)
hard	This material feels hard.	(1)
head	I'm not feeling very well today. My head aches.	(8)
headache	My brother has a bad headache.	(8)
healthy	My brother is healthy.	(8)
heavy	It's not too heavy, but I don't know the exact weight.	(1)

height	Do you happen to know Mr. Cooper's height and weight?	(3)
help	Would you help me lift this heavy box?	(2)
herself	She can't dress herself yet because she's too young.	(9)
high	Will you please measure this window to see how high it is?	(1)
himself	He can't dress himself yet because he's too young.	(9)
holiday	Mr. Cooper is happy because today is a holiday.	(10)
honest	Please give me your honest opinion.	(10)
hungry	I'm always hungry when I come home from work.	(9)
hurts	My right arm hurts.	(8)

I

idea	In my opinion, that's an excellent idea.	(10)
ill	I was ill yesterday, but I'm better today.	(8)
improvements	There have been a lot of improvements here in the last 20 years.	(5)
inches	The walls are three inches thick.	(1)
incorrect	What do you think? Is that incorrect?	(10)
information	Excuse me, sir. Can you give me some information?	(3)
interrupt	Please don't interrupt me now—I'm very busy.	(2)
into	Please pour this milk into that glass.	(2)

J

jacket	He tries to button his own jacket, but he can't do it.	(9)
judgment	Of course I want to know what your judgment is.	(10)
jump	I jump out of bed at about 7 o'clock every morning.	(9)

K

kind	Are your neighbors very kind?	(5)
kitchen	Get me a hammer from the kitchen, will you?	(2)
knee	I've got a pain in my knee.	(8)
knives	Please pick up those knives and forks, will you?	(2)
know	We all know each other pretty well.	(5)

L

ladies' room	Could you tell me where the nearest ladies' room is?	(3)
large	One of my suitcases is large, and the other one is medium size.	(1)
leave	Leave your books on the table, will you please?	(2)
leg	How did you break your leg?	(8)
length	That street is only two miles in length.	(1)
let . . . know	Would you please let him know that I'm here?	(2)
library	Take these books to the library with you tonight.	(2)
lift	Would you help me lift this heavy box?	(2)
light	My book has a light blue cover.	(1)
lighter	This pencil is lighter than that one.	(1)
lights	Please ask John to turn on the lights.	(2)

like	What was the weather like yesterday?	(7)
literature	I like geography, but I prefer literature.	(10)
living room	John goes downstairs to the living room.	(9)
long	How long is Jones Boulevard?	(1)
love	Personally, I love winter weather.	(10)

M

mailing	Would you mind mailing this letter for me?	(2)
married	Are you married?	(4)
marry	Who did George marry?	(4)
marvelous	In my opinion, that's a marvelous idea.	(10)
material	This material feels soft.	(1)
mathematics	I like geography, but I prefer mathematics.	(10)
matter	What's the matter with you?	(8)
measure	Will you please measure this window to see how wide it is?	(1)
medical	Please give me your medical opinion.	(10)
medicine	I like geography, but I prefer medicine.	(10)
medium	One of my suitcases is small, and the other one is medium size.	(1)
men's room	Could you tell me where the nearest men's room is?	(3)
miles	That street is only two miles long.	(1)
miserable	The weather was miserable last week.	(7)
miss	You can't miss it.	(3)
miss	Excuse me, miss.	(3)
mistaken	I think you're mistaken about that.	(10)
move	Would you help me move this heavy box?	(2)
moved in	A young married couple moved in next door to us.	(5)
music	I like geography, but I prefer music.	(10)
myself	I can't dress myself yet because I'm too young.	(9)

N

nail	Get me a nail from the kitchen, will you?	(2)
narrow	This narrow table weighs about forty-five pounds.	(1)
naturally	Naturally.	(10)
neck	I've got a pain in my neck.	(8)
nephew	I'm single, and my nephew is still single.	(4)
new	They're building a new house up the street from me.	(5)
nice	The weather is nice today.	(7)
niece	Your niece is engaged, isn't she?	(4)
noisy	Are your neighbors very noisy?	(5)
number	Do you happen to know Mr. Cooper's telephone number?	(3)

O

occupied	I beg your pardon. Is this seat occupied?	(3)
of course	Of course I want to know what your opinion is!	(10)
off	I get into bed at about 11:30, and go right off to sleep.	(9)

officer	Excuse me, Officer.	(3)
only	That street is only two miles long.	(1)
opinion	In my opinion, that's an excellent idea.	(10)
ounces	This book weighs twenty ounces.	(1)
ourselves	We can't dress ourselves yet because we're too young.	(9)
own	What size suitcase do you own?	(1)
own	He tries to button his own shirt, but he can't do it.	(9)

P

package	Would you mind mailing this package for me?	(2)
pain	I've got a pain in my back.	(8)
pajamas	At bedtime, I take off my clothes and put on my pajamas.	(9)
pants	He tries to button his own pants, but he can't do it.	(9)
pardon	I beg your pardon.	(3)
passed away	She's a widow. Her husband passed away last year.	(4)
perfect	The weather is perfect today.	(7)
personally	Personally, I prefer winter weather.	(10)
pet	What do you think of my pet dog?	(10)
pick up	Please pick up those cups and saucers.	(2)
pictures	Please count the pictures in that room.	(2)
place	Place your books on the table, will you please?	(2)
plates	Please pick up those plates and glasses, will you?	(2)
poem	What do you think of my poem?	(10)
post office	Can you tell me where the post office is?	(3)
pounds	This round table weighs about forty-five pounds.	(1)
pour	Please pour this milk into that glass.	(2)
prefer	Personally, I prefer winter weather.	(10)
probably	I'll probably wake up early and get up at 6:30.	(6)
profession	Do you happen to know Mr. Cooper's profession?	(3)
purchase	If you purchase that home, will you spend the rest of your life there?	(5)
put	Put your books on the table, will you please?	(2)
put back	Put my coat back in the closet, will you?	(2)
put down	Put your books down on the table.	(2)
put on	After brushing my teeth, I put on my clothes.	(9)

Q

quiet	Are your neighbors very quiet?	(5)

R

railroad	Can you tell me where the railroad station is?	(3)
raincoat	He tries to button his own raincoat, but he can't do it.	(9)
rained	Yesterday it rained all day.	(7)
ready	After breakfast, I'll get ready to go to work.	(6)
recommendation	Of course I want to know what your recommendation is.	(10)
religion	I like geography, but I prefer religion.	(10)
remind	Would you please remind him that I'm here?	(2)
rented	An elderly man rented the big white house.	(5)

reserved	I beg your pardon. Is this seat reserved?	(3)
round	This round table weighs about forty-five pounds.	(1)
rugs	Please count the rugs in that room.	(2)
ruler	Get me a ruler from the kitchen, will you?	(2)

S

sad	I'm always sad when I come home from work.	(9)
saucers	Please pick up those cups and saucers.	(2)
seat	I beg your pardon. Is this seat taken?	(3)
see	Will you please measure this window to see how wide it is?	(1)
shape	I like the shape of that table.	(1)
shave	Then, I shave, brush my teeth and comb my hair.	(9)
shoulder	I'm not feeling very well today. My left shoulder aches.	(8)
shower	After getting up, I go into the bathroom and take a shower.	(9)
sick	I was very sick yesterday, but I'm better today.	(8)
single	No, I'm not married. I'm still single.	(4)
sir	Excuse me, sir. Can you give me some information?	(3)
size	What size suitcase do you own?	(1)
sleepy	When I get sleepy, I'll probably get ready for bed.	(6)
sleet	It's going to sleet tomorrow.	(7)
slight	I've got a slight pain in my back.	(8)
slipped	I slipped on the stairs and fell down.	(8)
snow	It's going to snow tomorrow.	(7)
so	Why is Mr. Cooper so tired?	(10)
soft	This material feels soft.	(1)
soon	I hope you'll be well soon.	(8)
sore	Which of your arms is sore?	(8)
spend	If you buy that home, will you spend the rest of your life there?	(5)
spent	My friend spent his childhood in California.	(5)
spoons	Please pick up those spoons, will you?	(2)
spring	Today is the first day of spring.	(7)
square	This square table weighs about forty-five pounds.	(1)
stairs	The restaurant is up those stairs.	(3)
station	Can you tell me where the railroad station is?	(3)
stay	I'll probably stay home and watch television.	(6)
stomach	I've got a pain in my stomach.	(8)
store	There used to be a grocery store on this corner.	(5)
stormy	What was the weather like yesterday? Was it stormy?	(7)
story	What do you think of my story?	(10)
straight	It's two blocks straight ahead.	(3)
strong	There's a strong wind this evening, isn't there?	(7)
suitcase	What size suitcase do you own?	(1)
summer	Today is the first day of summer.	(7)
summertime	I like summertime best.	(10)

weigh	How much does that typewriter weigh?	(1)
weight	It's not too heavy, but I don't know the exact weight.	(1)
wet	This material feels wet.	(1)
whether	I don't know whether it will rain or not.	(10)
which of	Which of your arms is sore?	(8)
why	Why is Mr. Cooper so tired?	(10)
wide	Will you please measure this window to see how wide it is?	(1)
widow	She's a widow. Her husband died last year.	(4)
width	This window is two feet wide. What's the width of that window?	(1)
wind	There's a strong wind this evening, isn't there?	(7)
windy	It's windy today.	(7)
winter	Today is the first day of winter.	(7)
wonderful	In my opinion, that's a wonderful idea.	(10)
wrap	Would you help me wrap this heavy box?	(2)
wrist	How did you break your wrist?	(8)
wrong	What do you think? Is that wrong?	(10)

Y

yards	That street is only 300 yards long.	(1)
yardstick	Get me a yardstick from the kitchen, will you?	(2)
yourself	You can't dress yourself yet because you're too young.	(9)

Z

zero	The temperature is about zero degrees centigrade.	(7)

KEY

TO EXERCISES AND REVIEW LESSONS

UNIT 1

Page 9

1. *a.* 25 lbs., *b.* heavier, *c.* lighter, *d.* 36 feet, *e.* wider, *f.* width, *g.* narrower, *h.* thick

2. *a.* color, *b.* shape, *c.* weight, *d.* length, *e.* size , *f.* height, *g.* width, *h.* material

3. *a.* light, *b.* large, *c.* hard, *d.* narrow, *e.* dry, *f.* thin, *g.* short, *h.* thick, *i.* wide, *j.* heavy, *k.* soft, *l.* wet, *m.* long

4. *a.* What is the weight; *b.* How wide; *c.* How long; *d.* How thick; *e.* What is the width; *f.* How much heavier; *g.* What color; *h.* What sizes; *i.* What shape; *j.* What is the length; *k.* how tall

5. *a.* weigh, *b.* weigh, *c.* weighs, *d.* measure, *e.* measures, *f.* am, *g.* are, *h.* are, *i.* weigh, *j.* measuring, *k.* weighing, *l.* is , *m.* measuring, *n.* is, *o.* measure

UNIT 2

Page 20

1. *a.* turn . . . on; *b.* Put . . . down; *c.* Hang . . . up; *d.* wait for; *e.* doing . . . for; *f.* pick up; *g.* taking . . . back; *h.* turn . . . off

2. *a.* Would you please get me a hammer?
   b. Would you please count the chairs in this room?
   c. Would you please pour this milk into that glass?
   d. Would you please help me lift this heavy box?
   e. Would you please take these books home?
   f. Would you please turn the lights off?
   g. Would you please bring me those magazines?

3. *a.* help, *b.* helping, *c.* help, *d.* help, *e.* mail, *f.* mailing, *g.* mail, *h.* mail, *i.* hang, *j.* hanging, *k.* hang, *l.* hang

125

4. *a.* Don't wait for me at five o'clock.
    b. She won't have time to do me a favor.
    c. He didn't get me a glass of milk yesterday.
    d. Aren't you going to help me wrap this box?
    e. Don't bring me a yardstick.
    f. These nails don't weigh too much.
    g. I didn't turn off the radio.
    h. I'm not very busy.
    i. Don't pour me a cup of coffee.
    j. He didn't help me lift the heavy box.
    k. Don't count all the chairs in this room.
    l. He isn't bothering me.
    m. Isn't he talking to you?
    n. Don't take these magazines back to the library.
    o. Don't leave your books on the table.

UNIT 3

Page 30

1. *a.* way,   *b.* straight ahead,   *c.* far,   *d.* miss,   *e.* across,
    f. long drive,   *g.* miles,   *h.* taken,   *i.* right,   *j.* corner

2. *a.* Peach Street is two miles straight ahead.
    b. The bank is five miles from here.
    c. The nearest restaurant is across the street.
    d. You should go to the right at the next corner to get to the post office.
    e. The nearest telephone is in the men's room or the ladies' room.
    f. The school is in the middle of the next block.
    g. The railroad station is around the corner.
    h. The National Theater is right on the corner of Washington Street.
    i. It is a long drive from here to the airport.
    j. The university is about two miles to the left.

3. *a.* How far is the church from here?
    b. Where is the bank?
    c. Who is this seat reserved for?
    d. Whose address don't I know?
    e. Which way should we turn at the next corner?
    f. What is a short walk from the hotel?

g. What is around the corner?
h. Who gave me some information?
i. Which way is the National Theater?
j. Where is the telephone?
k. What time will the post office open?
l. How old is Mr. Cooper?
m. How far is the airport from the town?
n. When am I going to school?
o. How often is this table reserved for Mr. Cooper?
p. Whose telephone number is this?
q. Which seat is occupied?

UNIT 4

Page 40

1. a. grandparents,   b. aunt,   c. uncle,   d. cousin,   e. niece,
   f. nephew,   g. grandchildren,   h. brother,   i. sister
   j. grandmother,   k. grandfather,   l. husband

2. a. Our,   b. My,   c. your,   d. Their,   e. His,   f. Her

3. a. She's a widow. Her husband died last year.
   b. He's engaged to be married.
   c. They're going to have a baby.
   d. You're still single.
   e. They don't know when the wedding will be.
   f. She didn't get married last year.
   g. Mr. and Mrs. Cooper don't have any children but they'd like to.
   h. George isn't a bachelor; he's been married for a long time.
   i. I'm a bachelor, but I'd like to get married.
   j. They've been married for approximately three years.
   k. I'm going to get married in exactly three days.
   l. My sister's been engaged for two months.
   m. Today's my parents' anniversary.

4. a. Your nephew is engaged, isn't he?
   b. Your granddaughter got married in 1945, didn't she?
   c. You're still a bachelor, aren't you?
   d. They had a child last month, didn't they?
   e. Yesterday was your anniversary, wasn't it?
   f. They've been married for many years, haven't they?

g. She's been a widow since last year, hasn't she?
h. Mr. and Mrs. Cooper have several children, don't they? (haven't they?)
i. Your wedding will take place in June, won't it?
j. You're engaged now, aren't you?
k. Your niece is married, isn't she?
l. You got married last year, didn't you?

UNIT 5

Page 50

1. *a.* grow up, *b.* grew up, *c.* grow up, *d.* grew up, *e.* grow up, *f.* grows up
2. *a.* woke up, *b.* wake up, *c.* wakes up, *d.* woke up, *e.* woke up
3. *a.* spent, *b.* spend, *c.* spend, *d.* spent, *e.* spent
4. *a.* of, *b.* up, *c.* on, *d.* in, *e.* from, *f.* until, *g.* from, *h.* on, *i.* in, *j.* up
5. *a.* What a large building that is!
   b. What beautiful flowers those are!
   c. What quiet neighbors you have!
   d. What a happy childhood he had!
   e. What a noisy neighborhood this is!
   f. What a friendly couple that is!
6. *a.* he did, *b.* I did, *c.* she has, *d.* I don't, *e.* I am, *f.* he hasn't, *g.* she won't, *h.* she did, *i.* there have, *j.* they are

REVIEW ONE

Page 54

2. *a.* weigh, *b.* weighed, *c.* liked, *d.* feels, *e.* owned, *f.* have, *g.* measured, *h.* weighs, *i.* asked, *j.* bothering, *k.* hung up, *l.* wrapping, *m.* pouring, *n.* building, *o.* moved in, *p.* spent, *q.* buys, *r.* used to, *s.* grew up, *t.* bought, *u.* are, *v.* telling, *w.* is, *x.* got married, *y.* died, *z.* wants to

3.

No Key answers can be given for these exercises.

4.

UNIT 6

Page 64

1. *a.* left,   *b.* leave,   *c.* will leave,   *d.* went,   *e.* am going (go),
   f. will go,   *g.* was,   *h.* will be,   *i.* woke up,   *j.* will wake up,
   k. watched,   *l.* will watch

2. *a.* John'll probably wake up soon.
   b. He'll have breakfast after he wakes up.
   c. Then he'll get ready to go to work.
   d. After that, he'll leave the house.
   e. He'll read the newspaper on the way to work.
   f. John won't wake up in the middle of the night.
   g. He won't go out for breakfast.
   h. He won't leave the house before breakfast.
   i. He won't finish working until 5:30.
   j. He won't get home by 6:30.
   k. He'll get home at 7:00.
   l. He'll be able to eat dinner with us.
   m. Next, he'll probably watch television.
   n. After that, he'll go to sleep.

3. *a.* Do you think you'll finish reading the newspaper at 5:30?
   b. Do you think he got home by 6:00 yesterday?
   c. Do you think John'll go to the movies with us?
   d. Do you think she'll be able to go out for lunch?
   e. Do you think they woke up early yesterday morning?
   f. Do you think he used to leave the house at 8 o'clock?
   g. Do you think you'll be able to make some phone calls after breakfast?
   h. Do you think they wrote some letters after breakfast?
   i. Do you think we'll finish working at 5:30?
   j. Do you think I'll be able to get home by 6 o'clock?
   k. Do you think your friend went to sleep right away?
   l. Do you think John made some phone calls early this morning?
   m. Do you think she'll be ready to go to work right away?
   n. Do you think Mr. Cooper'll be able to eat dinner with us a week from today?

UNIT 7

Page 74

1. *a.* it did,   *b.* it isn't,   *c.* it is,   *d.* it hasn't,   *e.* it has,   *f.* it isn't,   *g.* it is,   *h.* it wasn't,   *i.* it doesn't,   *j.* there is, *k.* they are

2. *a.* hailed,   *b.* snowing,   *c.* hotter,   *d.* raining,   *e.* nice, *f.* drizzling,   *g.* wind,   *h.* cloudy,   *i.* cleared up,   *j.* terrible

	Student A	*Student B*
3. *a.*	It's cold today, isn't it?	Yes, it is.
b.	Today is the first day of spring, isn't it?	Yes, it is.
c.	There's a strong wind this evening, isn't there?	Yes, there is.
d.	The temperature will be about 70 degrees today, won't it?	Yes, it will.
e.	It'll probably clear up this afternoon, won't it?	Yes, it will.
f.	It's been cloudy all morning, hasn't it?	Yes, it has.
g.	The weather was miserable last week, wasn't it?	Yes, it was.
h.	It snowed all day yesterday, didn't it?	Yes, it did.
i.	It's been cold all winter, hasn't it?	Yes, it has.
j.	There was a terrible storm in New York, wasn't there?	Yes, there was.

4. *a.* It,   *b.* You,   *c.* There,   *d.* She,   *e.* We,   *f.* He, *g.* they,   *h.* I

UNIT 8

Page 84

1. *a.* don't,   *b.* is,   *c.* has,   *d.* hurts,   *e.* break,   *f.* slipped, *g.* slips,   *h.* hopes,   *i.* is,   *j.* broken,   *k.* hope to,   *l.* got, *m.* better,   *n.* swollen

2. *a.* sick,   *b.* coughing, sore throat,   *c.* had to,   *d.* matter, *e.* ached,   *f.* better,   *g.* pains

3. *a.* fell,   *b.* swollen, bleeding,   *c.* ought to,   *d.* hurts, *e.* break,   *f.* pain

4. *a.* I've got a terrible toothache.
   b. He's got a broken leg.
   c. You'd better see a doctor about that.
   d. She doesn't feel well this morning.
   e. He shouldn't go to work with a bad cold.
   f. I don't feel better today.
   g. My fever's gone.
   h. My arm's broken.

5. *a.* John doesn't have a fever.
   b. I haven't got a headache.
   c. I didn't hurt my leg when I fell down.
   d. Haven't you ever had a sore throat?
   e. Didn't you have a toothache yesterday?
   f. Aren't you feeling sick today?
   g. Shouldn't you see a doctor about that?
   h. Didn't she feel better this morning?

UNIT 9

Page 95

1. *a.* I get out of bed every morning about 7 o'clock.
   b. I brush my teeth after taking a shower.
   c. I go downstairs after I put on my clothes.
   d. I eat breakfast downstairs in the kitchen.
   e. My brother can't dress himself yet because he is too young.
   f. I feel tired and hungry when I come home from work.
   g. I put on my pajamas at bedtime.
   h. I get into bed about 11:30.

2. *a.* get out, *b.* getting up, *c.* put on, *d.* wake up, *e.* go into, *f.* take off, *g.* get into, *h.* go . . . off

3. *a.* My little brother still can't dress himself.
   b. My little brother can't bathe himself yet.
   c. I always get up at 7:00 every morning.
   d. He usually brushes his teeth after he shaves.
   e. He still hasn't combed his hair.
   f. He hasn't washed his face and hands yet.
   g. I'm always hungry when I wake up.
   h. I'm usually tired when I come home from work.

4. *a.* my,   *b.* his,   *c.* himself,   *d.* her,   *e.* herself,   *f.* them-
selves,   *g.* yourself,   *h.* their,   *i.* your,   *j.* they,   *k.* he,
l. we,   *m.* I (we),   *n.* she,   *o.* you

5. *a.* brush,   *b.* comb,   *c.* fix,   *d.* button,   *e.* shave,   *f.* wash,
g. take,   *h.* jump,   *i.* put,   *j.* take

UNIT 10

Page 107

1. *a.* Do you think it's going to rain tomorrow?
   b. Don't you think you're mistaken about that?
   c. Do you suppose Mr. Cooper was tired because he worked hard all day?
   d. Do you believe I'll enjoy the movie?
   e. Do you feel you can give me your honest opinion?
   f. Don't you feel Mr. Cooper is angry because he didn't have lunch today?
   g. Don't you believe Mr. Cooper is happy because today is his birthday?
   h. Don't you suppose Mr. Cooper prefers warm weather?
   i. Do you think she loves winter weather?
   j. Do you believe he worked hard all day?

2. *a.* I don't know whether it'll rain tomorrow or not.
   b. I don't know whether John will enjoy the movie or not.
   c. I don't know whether John will give you his honest opinion or not.
   d. I don't know whether I'll see Mr. Cooper next Sunday or not.
   e. I don't know whether she's mistaken about that or not.
   f. I don't know whether Mr. Cooper prefers warm weather or not.
   g. I don't know whether I'll finish working early today or not.
   h. I don't know whether she had lunch yet or not.
   i. I don't know whether John always eats good food or not.

3. *a.* judgment,   *b.* like,   *c.* wonderful,   *d.* wrong,   *e.* correct,
   f. Naturally

4. *a.* Yes, he is. No, he isn't.
   b. Yes, I do. No, I don't.
   c. Yes, I do. No, I don't.

d. Yes, she does. No, she doesn't.
e. Yes, you are. No, you aren't.
f. Yes, we are. No, we aren't.
g. Yes, he was. No, he wasn't.
h. Yes, we were. No, we weren't.
i. Yes, I did. No, I didn't.
j. Yes, I did. No, I didn't.
k. Yes, he does. No, he doesn't.
l. Yes, she is. No, she isn't.
m. Yes, you are. No, you aren't.
n. Yes, he is. No, he isn't.

REVIEW TWO

Page 110

1. a. I will (am going to) get up at 7 o'clock tomorrow.
b. I will (am going to) have breakfast at 9 o'clock tomorrow.
c. I will (am going to) go to the movies with a friend of mine tomorrow.
d. We will (are going to) have dinner at home tomorrow.
e. I will (am going to) get dressed quickly tomorrow.
f. I will (am going to) have toast and coffee for breakfast tomorrow.
g. My brother will (is going to) get up later than I will tomorrow.
h. I will (am going to) finish working at 5:30 in the afternoon tomorrow.
i. My sister will (is going to) go to sleep immediately tomorrow.
j. My parents will (are going to) leave the house at 10 o'clock tomorrow.
k. It will (is going to) rain all day tomorrow.
l. There will (is going to) be a cool breeze tomorrow.
m. It will (is going to) snow tomorrow.
n. I won't (am not going to) feel well tomorrow.
o. My little brother will (is going to) take a bath before he goes to bed tomorrow.
p. We will (are going to) be tired when we come home from work tomorrow.
q. Will it (Is it going to) rain tomorrow?
r. Will he (Is he going to) be sick tomorrow?
s. The weather will (is going to) be very nice tomorrow.

    t. She will (is going to) go out for lunch at 12 noon tomorrow.

    u. Will you (Are you going to) have dinner at home tomorrow?

    v. When I get sleepy tomorrow, I will (am going to) go to bed.

    w. After breakfast tomorrow, I will (am going to) get ready to go to work.

    x. Mrs. Cooper will (is going to) go to sleep at about 11:30 tomorrow.

    y. My brother will (is going to) wake up at 7 o'clock tomorrow.

    z. She will (is going to) get dressed at 6:30 tomorrow.

2. *a.* I won't get up at 6 o'clock tomorrow.

    b. My birthday will not be tomorrow.

    c. We won't have dinner at home tomorrow.

    d. I will not eat dinner at 8 p.m. tomorrow.

    e. I will not watch television for an hour tomorrow.

    f. We will not work from 9 a.m. until 5:30 p.m. tomorrow.

    g. Tomorrow I will not measure the windows to see how wide they are.

    h. I will not be able to go to sleep immediately tomorrow.

    i. They will not buy the house on the corner tomorrow.

    j. My cousin will not get married tomorrow.

3. *a.* Did you get up at 6 o'clock?

    b. Are you married yet?

    c. How long have they been married?

    d. Do they know when the wedding will be?

    e. Is the weather nice today?

    f. Is it raining now?

    g. What is the temperature this afternoon?

4.

    No Key answers can be given for these exercises.

5.